Men of Wisdom

SAINT PAUL

AND THE MYSTERY OF CHRIST

By

CLAUDE TRESMONTANT

Translated by

DONALD ATTWATER

NEW YORK	LONDON
HARPER AND BROTHERS	LONGMANS

CONTENTS

Scriptural quotations in this book are taken from the Knox Version of the Bible. Variations in references between the Knox and Authorized versions are shown in square brackets and, in addition, it should be noted that 1 Kings in the Knox Version is equivalent to 1 Samuel in the Authorized.

'The Mystical Mill':
St. Paul gathering the flour from the wheat
of the Old Law (Vezelay)

CHRONOLOGICAL TABLE

DATES	EVENTS	DOCUMENTS	LETTERS	CONTEMPORARY HISTORY
First years of the Christian era	Birth of Paul	Acts 7: 58 Philemon 9		Emperor Augustus 31 B.C.–A.D. 14
c. 36	Stoning of Stephen	Acts 7: 58, 9: 1		
	Paul's conversion	Acts 22: 4 Gal. 1: 13		
c. 36–39	He stays in Damascus, then in Arabia, then in Damascus again	Acts 9: 19 Gal. 1: 17 Acts 9: 23		Caligula, 37–41
c. 39	Visit to Jerusalem, and interview with Peter	Gal. 1: 18 Acts 9: 26		
c. 39–42	Visit to Tarsus	Acts 9: 30 Gal. 1: 21		
c. 43–44	Visit to Antioch	Acts 11: 25		Claudius 41–54 Herod Agrippa, king in Palestine, 41–44
c. 44	Famine; collection; visit to Jerusalem	Acts 11: 27 12: 25		
c. 45–49	First missionary journey	Acts 13 - 14		
49 or 50	Conference at Jerusalem	Acts 15: 1–35 Gal. 2: 1–10		Claudius expels the Jews from Rome
	Disagreement with Peter at Antioch	Gal. 2: 11–14		
50–53	Second missionary journey	Acts 15: 36 ff.	Thessalonians	Gallio procurator at Antioch
52 or 53	Third missionary journey	Acts 18: 23 ff.	Galatians	
57 or 58		Acts 21: 17 ff.	Corinthians Romans	Nero, 54–68
58–60	Imprisonment at Caesarea	Acts 24–26		Festus procurator in Judaea, 60–62
59–60	Taken prisoner to Rome	Acts 27, 28		
60 or 61 to ?	In captivity at Rome	Acts 28	Colossians Ephesians Philippians	
				Rome burnt, July 64
?	Journeys ?		Timothy Titus	Rising in Judaea, 66–70
?	Second imprisonment at Rome ?			
?	Death			Death of Nero, June 68

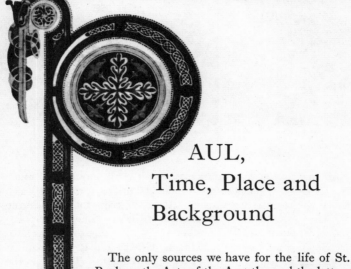

AUL,
Time, Place and
Background

The only sources we have for the life of St. Paul are the Acts of the Apostles and the letters he wrote to various Christian communities.

He was born in the early years of the Christian era, and so was a little younger than our Lord Jesus Christ. We read in Acts 7: 58 that at the time of the stoning of Stephen he was a 'young man' (*neanias*), and in his note to Philemon (9) he calls himself 'Paul, an old man' (*presbutes*).

His Hebrew name was *Shaul*, Saul, the name of the first king of Israel, and he was born at Tarsus in Cilicia: he tells us so himself, twice: 'I am a Jew, born at Tarsus in Cilicia' (Acts 22: 3); 'I am a Jew . . . a citizen of Tarsus in Cilicia, no mean city' (Acts 21: 39). According to St. Jerome, Paul's family originally came from Giskala in Galilee. Paul's father had become a freeman of Tarsus and a Roman citizen— it is not known how—and Paul himself was to appeal to his Roman citizenship when the occasion arose. This citizenship carried certain privileges with it: it was forbidden to inflict ignominious punishments on a *civis romanus*, and on a capital charge he could be tried only in the Roman imperial court.

Tarsus was a well-known place in those days. It stood at a

Initial letter from the Epistle to
the Romans in the Bible of
Charles the Bald

5

The Taurus Mountains

road junction at an entrance to the Taurus mountains, much nearer the sea than the present little Turkish town, and was a meeting-place of two worlds. It was perhaps founded during the last days of the Hittite empire; its name occurs on the obelisk of Shalmaneser III (9th century B.C.). The town was subject in turn to Assyrians, Persians, Greeks and Romans, and it became a melting-pot of cultures and religions. Thanks to the river Kydnos, it was a trading-port for all the Mediterranean basin, 'a big, prosperous city,' as Xenophon calls it. This mixture of peoples, languages, ways of life and social classes was a rich soil for young Saul to grow up in. It is important to remember that he was not born into a closed community in the Judaean countryside, but in a busy city, open to the sea, among representatives of many peoples: such a place was favourable to the growth of a feeling for universality.

But Tarsus was not only an important place commercially; it was also a cultural centre, able to compete, says Strabo, with Athens and Alexandria. Situated as it was at a meeting-place of

Tarsus from the south-west

East and West, of Semitic and Greek civilization, it was able to produce philosophers who were known all over the ancient world; it is again Strabo who writes, 'Rome is full of men from Tarsus and Alexandria,' and he names, among others, the stoic philosophers Athenodosius and Nestor. Religions of very diverse origin had brought about a syncretism in which native, Assyrian, Persian and Greek elements were mixed; side by side with Baal

Baal of Tarsus
(*Coin of 4th century* B.C.)

Tarz (the Lord of Tarsus) there was the young deity Sandan, who was later assimilated to the Greek Herakles. Every year the festival of the god of vegetation was observed: his image was first burnt, and then his return to life was celebrated, and in the rejoicings that followed the funeral ceremony there was no lack of debauchery. The mystery religions were represented too, notably by the cult of Mithras. And there was a Jewish colony, as in all important cities of the Roman empire.

Paul was a townsman by birth and upbringing. Jesus uses language and illustrations that belong to the country—the sower,

Tarsus: the West Gate

the fig-tree and its sprouting buds, the growth of trees, the colour of the sky, the shepherd's life, the vine; but Paul's comparisons and similes are those of the city: the stadium (1 Cor. 9: 24; Phil. 3: 14; 2 Tim. 4: 7 ff.); military life (1 Thess. 5: 8; Eph. 6: 10 ff.; Philemon 2; I Cor. 9: 7, 14: 8; 2 Cor. 2: 14, 10: 3; Phil. 2: 25; Col. 2: 15); seafaring (1 Tim. 1: 19); slavery (many references); the theatre, law-courts, commerce. There are no images taken from country life and work, and Paul has not got what used to be called the 'feeling for nature'; what he has got is a strong feeling for the human condition and life in society.

At the beginning of the Christian era Jewish people were to be found all over the Greco-Roman world, and even beyond it. The successive Assyrian and Babylonian deportations after the year 722, followed by spontaneous emigration, had brought about the dispersion (*diaspora*) of Israel. It was at the same time a sowing of seed: the Law of Moses (*Torah*) was carried beyond the frontiers of the Promised Land. The seeding of Israel all

House-building

A show in the Circus

Carding wool

Money-changers

Loading a ship

over the ancient world was a preparation for the spreading of the Gospel. In the time of the Maccabees, the Hebraic Sibyl told the Jewish people: 'You are everywhere, in every land and across every sea. All people will take offence at your customs.' Strabo, writing in the age of Augustus, said that the Jews had 'already spread to every town; there is not a place in the world they have not reached and made their influence felt', and there are plenty of documents and monuments to confirm the fact of this expansion. It is believed that there were a million Jews in Egypt and Syria, half a million in Palestine, and at least a million and a half in the rest of the empire.

Jerusalem continued to be the political and religious centre of this scattered people, and every year thousands of Jews journeyed there for the Passover and to bring their offering. Some of these pilgrims remained in the city, and so were formed the communities of 'foreign' Jews; one of them, called 'the Hellenists' or 'Grecians', is mentioned in Acts 6: 1. Throughout the *diaspora* the Jews taxed themselves on behalf of the upkeep of the Temple at Jerusalem, and every town had its alms-box for the safe keeping of this money till it was forwarded. Paul was to adopt this system in favour of the poor of Jerusalem at a time of special need. Regulations belonging to the time of Augustus show that the Jews were authorized to collect and transmit money in this way; and the Jews of the *diaspora* were granted certain juridical privileges: they had freedom of worship and were not constrained to observe the imperial cults. The commonest occupation of these Jews was agriculture: a number of monuments in Egypt and Asia Minor testify to the existence of colonies of them owning landed estates. Their industries were flourishing too, especially weaving and dyeing. Except at Alexandria, their activity in commerce was very secondary.

One of the characteristics of Judaism in the *diaspora* was *proselytism*. Our Lord says of the Pharisees that they 'encompass sea and land to gain a single proselyte' (Matt. 23: 15), and in one of his Satires (i, 4, 142) Horace makes allusion to it. Judaism felt called to become a world-wide religion, and its efforts in this direction had considerable success, uniting round the Synagogue those who feared God, that is, those who adhered to monotheism, accepted the obligations of Jewish morality, and observed the rules concerning the Sabbath and forbidden foods. Some went so far as to be circumcised, and these were the proselytes proper, who undertook to observe the whole Law; they thus became members of the people of Israel—but not children of Abraham.

Little has survived to us of Hellenistic Judaism. To borrow Lietzmann's phrase, in his *History of the Early Church*, Talmudic Judaism killed its brother, Greek-speaking Judaism. All we have of that rich culture now are some ruined synagogues and burying-grounds, a few inscriptions, some fragments of papyrus and parchment. As for literary remains, there is the Old Testament in Greek, the works of Josephus and Philo, some apocrypha, and the fragments of hellenistic Jewish writing preserved by Eusebius of Caesarea (*Praeparatio evangelica*, ix, 17–39) and by Clement of Alexandria (*Stromata*, i). The Bible was translated into Greek (the Septuagint) for the use of the community at Alexandria between the fourth and second centuries B.C., for the whole Mediterranean *diaspora* spoke Greek, the universal language of those days.

Greek manuscript of the Old Testament 2nd–1st century B.C. (Papyrus Fuad 266)

*Greek text from
Deuteronomy in the
Septuagint, 2nd century
B.C. (John Rylands
Library)*

When the exiles came back from Babylon they had brought
with them the common Eastern language, Aramaic, which was
spoken in Palestine for a thousand years. Hebrew remained the
sacred tongue and the language of scholarship, but the people
soon ceased to understand it properly, and it became the
speciality of the man of the Book, the scribe. So the sacred text
had to be translated for the purposes of worship and teaching,
and these oral translations into Aramaic—accompanied by commentaries—were the origin of the *Targums*. But in the *diaspora*,
teaching was given in the synagogue in Greek; in that tongue the
Bible was read and prayer and confession of faith made. However, that did not necessarily exclude a first liturgical reading in
Hebrew, followed by the translation. Preaching and exposition
of the Scriptures were also, of course, in Greek. Thus the
diaspora developed a Greek *Mishnah*, of which some idea may
be obtained from the writings of Paul, Philo and Josephus.

Paul learned Greek at Tarsus, it was his mother tongue:
popular Greek, the 'common tongue' (*koine*) used by traders and
sailors and soldiers. He read the Bible in the Septuagint translation, and this is important, for it means that certain Pauline
interpretations are not based on the Hebrew text but on this
translation, which sometimes differs noticeably. The Septuagint
is, in fact, not simply a translation: it also represents a development of biblical theology and shows a certain adaptation to
Greek ways of thinking.

It is unlikely that Paul was educated in a Greek school, but it is certain that he received a strict Jewish training in a family observant of the straitest Pharisaism. 'Saul, whose other name is Paul,' stoutly declares that he is 'a Pharisee, and my fathers were Pharisees before me' (Acts 13: 9, 23: 6): 'If others put their trust in outward claims, I can do so with better reason. I was circumcised seven days after I was born; I come from the stock of Israel, from the tribe of Benjamin, Hebrew-speaking as my parents were before me. Over the law, I was a Pharisee; to prove my loyalty, I persecuted the Church of God; in observing what the law commands, I was beyond reproach.' But (now he has become a Christian) what 'once stood to my credit, I now write down as loss, for the love of Christ' (Phil. 3: 4–7).

There were several parties, sects or 'schools' in the Judaism of those days. 'At that time,' writes Josephus, and he means the time of Jonathan (1 Macc. 12), 'at that time there were among the Jews three sects, which looked at human things in different ways. They were called Pharisees, Sadducees and Essenes. . . . The Pharisees imposed the obligation of observing certain points that are not written in the laws of Moses, but as handed down in the tradition of the fathers. The Sadducees rejected this obligation, holding that only written matters are binding, not those that depend on custom. Much study was given to this question, and it provoked great controversy. The Sadducean point of view appealed to the well-off, while the Pharisees had the mass of the people on their side. . . . So great was the Pharisees' authority with the people, that they were believed at once, even when they spoke against the king and the high priest' (*Antiquities of the Jews*, xiii, 5, 9; 10, 5).

The priests and the scribes were the preponderant elements in the historical development of Judaism after the exile. In the time of Ezra, they were still essentially at one, but from the beginning of the Hellenistic era they became more and more opposed till, in Maccabean times, they constituted two distinct parties. The Sadducees arose among the priests, the Pharisees among the scribes, but their disagreement was at different levels: the Pharisees were a religious party, of the strict observance, the

Sadducees were the aristocrats. The essence of Pharisaism was in its attitude towards the Law; the Sadducees were defined by social position, and after the destruction of Jerusalem by the Romans their influence came to an end: all subsequent Judaism has derived from Pharisaism. It has also influenced the theology of the Christian Church, for on dogmatic questions Jesus Christ expressly supported the Pharisees.

The word 'Pharisee' (Hebrew *parushim*, Aramaic *parishin*) means 'set apart'. The expression is uncommon in the Mishnah and no doubt it was a nickname, which in the end the Pharisees accepted. Set apart they were, in the sense that they tried to observe the Law more zealously and integrally than the general run of people, who from that very fact were looked on as insufficiently perfected, 'impure'. The Pharisees sought fully to understand the Law, to apply it strictly, and to adapt its requirements to cases not originally envisaged, so that a casuistry developed, and a jurisprudence was necessary for the multitudinous occasions when the authority of the Law had to be exercised. The Pharisees maintained that this jurisprudence was as binding as the written Law itself, whereas the Sadducees refused to recognize this addition to the laws of Moses. As for theology, the Pharisees had accepted the dogmatic 'development' since the book of Daniel, represented by belief in the resurrection of the dead; this the Sadducees would not accept, as not being expressed in the previous books. In the same way the Pharisees professed, and the Sadducees rejected, the doctrine of angelic spirits and of retribution after death. Christianity and later Judaism are the heirs of Pharisaic teaching on these matters.

Practically nothing is known about the education of a young *diaspora* Jew at this period, except that the father of a family was expressly bound himself to instruct his children in religion (Deut. 6: 7, 20). No doubt the Jewish communities were by now organizing elementary schools, the existence of which is certain at the epoch of the Mishnah, the second century A.D. at the latest. Philo writes: 'Since (the Jews) believe their laws to be revealed by God and are taught them from early childhood, the prescriptions of these laws are imprinted in their hearts.'

And Josephus: 'Above all are we concerned with the education of children. It is our pride to bring them up to the observance of the laws and religious practices which have been handed down to us in accordance with those laws: they are the most important things in life.' Josephus says elsewhere: 'Ask the first person you meet among us about the laws, and he will tell you them all as easily as his own name. A deep study of these laws from the very dawn of reason engraves them, as it were, on our minds.'

Elementary education was already widespread in the age of the Maccabees, when there was a rule that on the Sabbath day the superintendent of the synagogue (*hazzan*) should teach children to read; and there seems to have been a multiplication of primary schools during the first two centuries A.D. So young Saul certainly learned Hebrew as a child; and as soon as he knew the alphabet he will have begun to read the Bible, in the little parchment rolls (*megilloth*) that contain passages from the Pentateuch. A beginning was made with Leviticus, and the child had to learn a paragraph or verse by heart every day.

At the same time as he began to read God's written word and to learn the traditions of his forefathers, Saul must also have begun to learn his father's trade. 'To be solely concerned with the Torah, to the exclusion of following a trade, is to act like a man who knows not God.' So spoke a rabbi, for in Israel it was not as it was among the Greeks, who were contemptuous of manual work and left it to slaves. The Jewish doctors of the Law learned a trade in order to make a living. In the second century A.D. a rabbi said: 'Study of the Torah goes well with working at a trade, for the simultaneous exercise of these activities drives away sin: all study that is not accompanied by other work conduces to laziness and irregularity.' St. Paul will urge upon the communities that he has founded that every man shall 'work instead, and earn by his own labour the blessings he will be able to share with those who are in need' (Eph. 4: 28).

According to the doctors in Israel, then, a father's first duty to his son, after having him circumcised, is to teach him the Torah and then give him a trade. Manual work is looked on as a religious activity, and it must accompany study, 'following the example of rabbi Joshua ben Meshulam and rabbi Simeon ben Manasseh, who devoted a third of the day to the Torah, a third to prayer, and a third to work'. At the time of the Mishnah, and even earlier, nearly all teachers worked at a trade: Hillel and rabbi Aqiba were woodmen, rabbi Yohanan a shoemaker, rabbi Joshua ben Hanania a nailer. Such was the example of 'the holy rabbis of the land of Israel'.

Rabbi Saul was a tent-maker, in accordance with a tradition, commonly observed, that a man should follow his father's trade. And the fact that Paul was sent to study at Jerusalem suggests that his father was in easy circumstances.

THE FORMATIVE YEARS

Saul was probably about fifteen years old when he went away to Jerusalem. 'I am a Jew,' he says, 'born at Tarsus in Cilicia and brought up in this city [Jerusalem]. I was trained, under Gamaliel, in exact knowledge of our ancestral law . . .' (Acts 22: 3). The first thing taught was the sacred Scripture—the 'written law'. The word *torah* means instruction, but instruction which has got to be translated into reality, into action, 'lived'. Side by side with the written law that goes back to Moses, traditional,

Tent-making at Tarsus today, little changed since Paul's time

Scrolls of the Torah

Pharisaic, Judaism puts the 'oral torah', which has the same authority. For orthodox Judaism, the oral law (which was gradually codified) comes from Moses no less than does the written law: this too he received on Sinai, and it was transmitted by word of mouth to Joshua, from him to the elders, from the elders to the prophets, and so to the doctors and teachers. Its authority depends on its Mosaic origin, and its function is to complete and interpret the written law. For it to be effective in new circumstances arising in the course of history, the Torah of Moses had to be interpreted, clarified and developed, and tradition assigns this work in the first place to Ezra. Ezra, 'the priest . . . a scribe

17

well versed in the Lord's utterances, all the commands and observances he enjoined upon Israel, . . . his was a heart given up to study (*lidrosh*) of the Lord's law, ready to hold fast by it and teach the men of Israel decree and award' (Ezra 7: 11, 10). The levites 'read out the book of the law clear and plain, to give the sense of it, so that all could understand the reading' (Nehemiah 8: 7–8). This work of exegesis, the scrutinizing or searching of the written text in order to draw out its deepest meaning and practical applications, is called *midrash*. The Torah of Moses is both a history and a law, and the work of exegesis accordingly has a twofold aspect: the formation of a jurisprudence, the continual readapting of rules of life (*midrash halakah*); and the interpretation of the narrative parts of the Scripture (*midrash haggadah*). The two torahs therefore go together: that which is oral is God's explanation and development of that which is written.

So for over fifteen years Saul devoted himself to the study of the Bible and of its traditional interpretation, 'at the feet of Gamaliel'. This is no figure of speech: the student literally sat on the ground at his master's feet. The book of Acts tells us that the Pharisee Gamaliel was a doctor of the Law whom the people held in high regard, and it is worth the reader's while to re-read the passage in the Acts (5: 25–40) where he intervenes on behalf of the accused Apostles. Jewish tradition has preserved some of Gamaliel's 'sayings' and tells us that, when the old man died, 'the glory of the Torah came to an end, clean and temperate living was extinguished'.

Traditional Jewish studies called for much more memory work than does modern pedagogy. The student learnt the rabbis' maxims and sayings by heart, singing them over and over in a rhythmic chant. It is still possible to meet rabbis who have thus learnt by heart, not only all the Hebrew Bible, but much of the traditional commentaries as well. To facilitate such feats of memory, the rabbis elaborated mnemonic systems; they also emphasized the great importance of chanted repetition, lest one 'reads the Bible without making its melodiousness felt and studies the Mishnah without singing what it says'. 'Do you, acute one,

Hebrew Bible:
the Decalogue, Ex. 20: 2,
Deut. 5: 6; 2nd–1st century B.C.
(Nash papyrus, Cambridge
University)

read the Bible with open mouth, study the Mishnah with open mouth, so that the fruit of your work may remain with you' (*Berakhoth*, 36a). Oral teaching was not only chanted, the body too was moved in time with it: 'Is it not taught that if, during study, you move the 248 members of your body, you will remember what you learn, which otherwise is forgotten?' With such 'organic' memorizing, the prodigious memories of the Palestinian rabbis of the traditional school are no matter for surprise.

It should be remarked, too, that Talmudic teaching—whose methods may be assumed to have been in use in St. Paul's day—made systematic pedagogical use of interrogation, in a way that recalls Socratic usage and the Stoic *diatribe*: master questions pupil, and the pupil in turn has to ask questions to elicit explanations. There are not a few traces of this in Paul's letters (*e.g.*, Rom. chs. 3 and 4), the introduction of fictitious dialogue, expressing questions and doubts which lead to clearer explanations.

Paul retained certain features of his rabbinical training, a technique in the way of approaching and interpreting Scripture, and an aggregate of themes common to post-biblical Judaism or peculiar to Pharisaism. How much did Paul (and, more generally, the whole New Testament) owe to Judaism? This is a fundamental question, and so far it has not been answered exhaustively and satisfactorily. Nevertheless it is a field whose examination is of capital importance for the understanding of the New Testament and of the beginnings of Christian thought. The more one reads Paul and considers, however cursorily, what is known of the Judaism of his time, the more clear becomes the importance of the part that rabbinical speculations had in his thought: it must never be forgotten that he was a converted rabbi.

This question calls for a careful consideration, for which there is no space here. So far as Paul's exegetical processes are concerned, there may simply be recalled the *midrashim* of the letter to the Galatians (ch. 3) on the justification of Abraham, and of the letter to the Romans (ch. 4) on the same subject; on Sarah and Hagar in Galatians (ch. 4); on Moses' veil in 2 Corinthians (3: 7 ff.); the typology of Exodus in 1 Corinthians (ch. 10) ('that rock was Christ'); and especially the great *midrashim* of Romans (chs. 9 and 11), on the promise made to Abraham. St. Matthew's gospel and the letter to the Hebrews contain many examples of the same midrashic method.

For the rabbinical themes taken up by St. Paul, one example will suffice, that of Adam (cf. the typology of Adam in Rom. 5: 12). No notice was taken of this subject in the earliest scriptural thought, because in the Hebrew Bible the word *adam* simply means 'man', and in most of the texts is taken as a common noun. It is only in late writings (Wisdom 2: 24, 10: 1; Ecclus. 49: 19) and in post-biblical Jewish tradition, that Adam is read as a proper noun, and speculations about the first Adam and the second Adam become possible.

Pauline eschatology is also beholden to Judaism, and so are other matters that cannot be enumerated here.

To sum up this brief sketch of the formative influences of St. Paul's early years: his home was in Tarsus, a big, cosmopolitan, commercial city, amid a variety of languages, of ways of life, of religious and philosophical traditions; he belonged to a prosperous artisan family of Jews, strict Pharisees; and he was given a rabbinical training at Jerusalem.

Did Paul make any special study of pagan philosophy and the mystery religions? It is highly improbable: a God-fearing Jew did not defile himself by contact with heathen cults. If he sometimes uses the terminology of Stoic philosophy (which was then 'in the air') and of the mystery religions, this means no more than that he had picked up ideas and expressions that were common coin in such a place as Tarsus. When, writing to the Colossians, who were full of esoteric doctrines, he lards his language with mystical terms, that is one more example of his missionary method—to be 'all things to all men', that as many as possible might be saved. He may sometimes use the philosophical or religious language of his Hellenic surroundings, but his *thought* is integrally and exclusively biblical. For Paul, vocabulary is a garment, to be put on and off.

Nothing is known about his personal appearance. The description of him given in such an historically worthless writing as the *Acts of Paul* cannot be relied on. But in iconography, whose first reliable elements date from the fourth century, there is a certain consistency in the type of face given to him, which suggests a pretty firm tradition. On this subject, G. Wilpert's *Le pitture delle catacombe romane* (Rome, 1903) may be profitably consulted.

A word must be said about St. Paul's physical health. In the first place, his remarkable record of travelling must be borne in mind. These journeys were most often on foot, and in conditions which he describes himself in his second letter to the Corinthians (11: 23–28). It has been calculated that in his first missionary journey he travelled about 650 miles, in the second 875, and in the third, well over 1000, without counting other journeys before and after. And all the time working to pay his way, preaching the Good News, suffering beatings and

Saint Paul
Fresco in the Catacomb of Domitilla
c. 348

imprisonment, 'in danger from rivers, in danger from robbers, in
danger from my own people, in danger from the Gentiles;
danger in cities; danger in the wilderness, danger in the sea,
danger among false brethren! I have met with toil and weariness,
so often been sleepless, hungry and thirsty, so often denied
myself food, gone cold and naked.' He speaks of an infirmity
of the flesh (Gal. 4: 13–14), about which the Galatians were
not unsympathetic; and elsewhere (2 Cor. 12: 7) he refers to

Saint Paul
6th century ivory in the
Cluny Museum

Roman road from Aleppo to Antioch

a thorn in his flesh, but that does not necessarily mean a physical sickness. As we shall see, 'flesh' in the Bible signifies a person in his wholeness, and Paul's affliction may have been moral.*

Exegetes have reared some wonderful structures on these few data: the fact is that nothing certain and exact is known.

We first meet Paul as a young man, at Stephen's martyrdom. 'The witnesses put down their clothes at the feet of a young man named Saul. Thus they stoned Stephen; he, meanwhile, was praying: "Lord Jesus," he said, "receive my spirit;" and then, kneeling down, he cried aloud, "Lord, do not count this sin against them." And with that, he fell asleep. . . .' Saul approved of this execution, and afterwards he 'was making havoc of the church; he made his way into house after house, carrying men and women off and committing them to prison' (Acts 7: 57–60, 8: 3).

THE ROAD TO DAMASCUS

There are three accounts of Paul's conversion from Judaism to Christ. They are all given here, so that they may be compared and their common elements noted.

*For another view see: E. B. Allo: *Seconde Epitre aux Corinthiens*.

24

Saul, with every breath he drew, still threatened the disciples of the Lord with massacre: and now he went to the high priest and asked him for letters of commendation to the synagogues at Damascus, so that he could arrest all those he found there, men and women, who belonged to the way, and bring them back to Jerusalem. Then, on his journey, when he was nearly at Damascus, a light from heaven shone suddenly about him. He fell to the ground, and heard a voice saying to him, 'Saul, Saul, why dost thou persecute me?' 'Who art thou, Lord?' he asked. And he said, 'I am Jesus, whom Saul persecutes. . . . Rise up, and go into the city, and there thou shalt be told what thy work is.' His companions stood in bewilderment, hearing the voice speak, but not seeing anyone. When he rose from the ground he could see nothing, although his eyes were open, and they had to lead him by the hand, to take him into Damascus. Here for three days he remained without sight, and neither ate nor drank.

There was, in Damascus, a disciple named Ananias; to him the Lord called in a vision, 'Ananias.' 'Here I am, Lord,' he answered. And the Lord said to him, 'Rise up and go to the road called Straight Street; and enquire at the house of Judas

Martyrdom of Saint Stephen (Bourges).
'The witnesses put down their clothes at the feet of a
young man named Saul' (Acts 7: 57)

*'He fell to the ground, and heard a voice saying to him,
Saul, Saul, why dost thou persecute me?' (Acts 9: 4).
(Palatine Chapel at Palermo)*

for a man of Tarsus, named Saul. Even now he is at his prayers;
and he has had a vision of a man called Ananias coming in and
laying hands on him, to cure him of blindness.' At this,
Ananias answered, 'Lord, many have told me about this man,
and all the hurt he has done to thy saints at Jerusalem; and he
has come here with authority from the chief priests to imprison
all those who call upon thy name.' But the Lord said to him,
'Go on thy errand; this is a man I have chosen to be the instrument for bringing my name before the heathen and their rulers,
and before the people of Israel too. I have yet to tell him how
much suffering he will have to undergo for my name's sake.'

So Ananias set out; and as soon as he came into the house he laid his hands upon him, and said, 'Brother Saul, I have been sent by that Lord Jesus who appeared to thee on thy way as thou camest here; thou art to recover thy sight, and be filled with the Holy Spirit.' And with that, a kind of film fell away from his eyes, and his sight was recovered. He rose up, and was baptized; and now, when he had taken food, his strength returned to him. For some days he lived with the disciples at Damascus, and from the first, in the synagogues, he preached that Jesus was the Son of God.

All those who heard it were amazed; 'Why,' they said, 'is not this the man who brought ruin on all those who invoked this name, when he was in Jerusalem; the man who came here for the very purpose of arresting such people and presenting them to the chief priests?' But Saul was inspired with ever greater strength, and silenced the Jews who lived at Damascus by shewing them clearly that this was the Christ. (Acts 9: 1–22)

Straight Street, Damascus

The second account is put into Paul's own mouth. He is addressing the crowd at the time of his arrest in Jerusalem, in the year 58 or 59.

I am a Jew, born at Tarsus in Cilicia and brought up in this city; I was trained, under Gamaliel, in exact knowledge of our ancestral law, as jealous for the honour of the law as you are, all of you, to-day. I persecuted this way to the death, putting men and women in chains and handing them over to the prisons. The chief priests and all the elders will bear me out in that; it was from them that I was carrying letters to their brethren, when I was on my way to Damascus, to make fresh prisoners there and bring them to Jerusalem for punishment.

While I was on my journey, not far from Damascus, about midday, this befell me; all at once a great light from heaven shone about me, and I fell to the ground, and heard a voice saying to me, 'Saul, Saul, why dost thou persecute me?' 'Who art thou, Lord?' I answered. And he said to me, 'I am Jesus of Nazareth, whom Saul persecutes.' My companions saw the

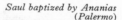

Saul baptized by Ananias
(Palermo)

He preached Christ in the synagogues (Acts 9: 20).
(Palermo)

light, but could not catch the voice of him who spoke to me.
Then I said, 'What must I do, Lord?' And the Lord said to
me, 'Rise up, and go into Damascus; there thou shalt be told
of all the work that is destined for thee.'

The glory of that light had blinded me, and my companions
were leading me by the hand when I came into Damascus.
There a certain Ananias, a man well known among his Jewish
neighbours for his pious observance of the law, came and stood
beside me, and said, 'Brother Saul, look up and see.' And at
that instant I looked up into his face. Then he said to me,

'The God of our fathers has made choice of thee to know his will, to have sight of him who is Just, and hear speech from his lips; and what thou hast seen and heard, thou shalt testify befor all men. Come then, why art thou wasting time? Rise up, and receive baptism, washing away thy sins at the invocation of his name.'

Afterwards, when I had gone back to Jerusalem, and was at prayer in the temple, I fell into a trance, and saw the Lord there speaking to me; 'Make haste,' he said, 'leave Jerusalem with all speed; they will not accept thy witness of me here.' 'But, Lord,' I said, 'it is within their own knowledge, how I used to imprison those who believed in thee, and scourge them in the synagogues; and when the blood of Stephen, thy martyr, was shed, I too stood by and gave my consent, and watched over the garments of those who slew him.'

And he said to me, 'Go on thy way; I mean to send thee on a distant errand, to the Gentiles.' (Acts 22: 3–21)

The third account is also Paul's own, before King Agrippa in the court of the procurator Festus (in the year 60). He has been invited to speak on his own behalf in answer to the charges brought by the Jews.

What my life was like when boyhood was over, spent from the first among my own people and in Jerusalem, all the Jews know; their earliest memory of me, would they but admit it, is of one who lived according to the strictest tradition of observance we have, a Pharisee. And if I stand here on my trial, it is for my hope of the promise God made to our fathers. Our twelve tribes worship him ceaselessly, night and day, in the hope of attaining that promise; and this is the hope, my lord king, for which the Jews call me to account. Why should it be beyond the belief of men such as thou art, that God should raise the dead?*

Well then, I thought it my duty to defy, in many ways, the name of Jesus the Nazarene. And that is what I did, at Jerusalem; it was I, under powers granted me by the chief priests, who shut up many of the faithful in prison; and when they were

---

* Here Paul is dividing his accusers: the Sadducees denied the resurrection of the dead, contrary to the Pharisees.

done to death, I raised my voice against them. Often have I tried to force them into blaspheming, by inflicting punishment on them in one synagogue after another; nay, so unmeasured was my rage against them that I used to go to foreign cities to persecute them.

It was on such an errand that I was making my way to Damascus, with powers delegated to me by the chief priests, when, journeying at midday, I saw, my lord king, a light from heaven, surpassing the brightness of the sun, which shone about me and my companions. We all fell to the ground, and I heard a voice which said to me, in Hebrew,* 'Saul, Saul, why dost thou persecute me? This is a thankless task of thine, kicking against the goad.'

'Who art thou, Lord?' I asked. And the Lord said, 'I am Jesus, whom Saul persecutes. Rise up, and stand on thy feet; I have shewn myself to thee, that I may single thee out to serve me, as the witness of this vision thou hast had, and other visions thou wilt have of me. I will be thy deliverer from the hands of thy people, and of the Gentiles, to whom I am now sending thee. Thou shalt open their eyes, and turn them from darkness to light, from the power of Satan to God, so that they may receive, through faith in me, remission of their sins and an inheritance among the saints.

Whereupon, king Agrippa, I did not shew myself disobedient to the heavenly vision. . . . (Acts 26: 4–19)

'I am Jesus, whom Saul persecutes.' Jesus is persecuted in the person of his community, his church; when Saul persecutes the Lord's followers, he persecutes the Lord himself. Here, in these words of Christ, Paul for the first time experiences the identity of the Lord with his Church, which is his Body. 'Where two or three are gathered together in my name, I am there in the midst of them' (Matt. 18: 20). Paul, no less than the Apostles, had seen the Risen Lord:

Here, brethren, is an account of the gospel I preached to you. It was this that was handed on to you; upon this your faith rests; through this (if you keep in mind the tenor of its preaching) you are in the way of salvation; unless indeed your belief was ill

---

* That is, in Aramaic.

founded. The chief message I handed on to you, as it was handed on to me, was that Christ, as the scriptures had foretold, died for our sins; that he was buried, and then, as the scriptures had foretold, rose again on the third day. That he was seen by Cephas, then by the eleven apostles, and afterwards by more than five hundred of the brethren at once, most of whom are alive at this day, though some have gone to their rest. Then he was seen by James, then by all the apostles; and last of all, I too saw him, like the last child, that comes to birth unexpectedly. Of all the apostles, I am the least; nay, I am not fit to be called an apostle, since there was a time when I persecuted the church of God; only, by God's grace, I am what I am, and the grace he has shewn me has not been without fruit; I have worked harder than all of them, or rather, it was not I, but the grace of God working with me. That is our preaching, mine or theirs as you will; that is the faith which has come to you. (1 Cor. 15: 1–11)

This passage is the oldest written testimony to Christ's resurrection that we have.

Paul often repeats that he has been called by God, that he has seen Christ, and that he is commissioned to be an apostle, 'one sent', not by men, but by the Lord himself. 'It is Paul who writes; a servant of Jesus Christ, called to be his apostle, and set apart to preach the gospel of God. That gospel, promised long ago by means of his prophets in the holy scriptures, tells us of his Son . . .' (Rom. 1: 1–2). 'Paul, whom the will of God has called to be an apostle of Jesus Christ . . .' (1 Cor. 1: 1); 'Paul, by God's will an apostle of Jesus Christ . . .' (2 Cor. 1:1); 'Paul, an apostle not holding his commission from men, not appointed by man's means, but by Jesus Christ, and God the Father who raised him from the dead . . .' (Gal. 1: 1). What he preaches, that he has received directly from the Lord: 'Am I not an apostle, have I not seen our Lord Jesus Christ?' (1 Cor. 9: 1); it is he who has given Paul the knowledge of the Mystery of Christ that he is to teach:

Let me tell you this, brethren; the gospel I preached to you is not a thing of man's dictation; it was not from man that I inherited or learned it, it came to me by a revelation from Jesus

Christ. You have been told how I bore myself in my Jewish days, how I persecuted God's church beyond measure and tried to destroy it, going further in my zeal as a Jew than many of my own age and race, so fierce a champion was I of the traditions handed down by my forefathers.

And then, he who had set me apart from the day of my birth, and called me by his grace, saw fit to make his Son known in me, so that I could preach his gospel among the Gentiles. My first thought was not to hold any consultations with any human creature; I did not go up to Jerusalem to see those who had been apostles longer than myself; no, I went off into Arabia, and when I came back, it was to Damascus. Then, when three years had passed, I did go up to Jerusalem, to visit Peter, and I stayed a fortnight there in his company; but I did not see any of the other apostles, except James, the Lord's brother. (Gal. 1: 11–19)

Immediately after his conversion, then, Paul withdrew into Arabia, that is, as defined by Josephus, the Nabataean kingdom east and south of Palestine, from the Red Sea to the Euphrates region. The book of Acts of the Apostles says nothing about his stay there, but it does tell us in what circumstances he had to leave Damascus:

So many days passed, and then the Jews plotted against his life. Saul was aware of the plot; and, since they kept watch over the gates, day and night, to make an end of him, the disciples contrived to let him down by night along the face of the wall, lowering him to the ground in a hamper.

So he reached Jerusalem, where he tried to attach himself to the disciples; but they could not believe he was a true disciple, and all avoided his company. Whereupon Barnabas took him by the hand and brought him in to the apostles, telling them how, on his journey, he had seen the Lord and had speech with him, and how at Damascus he had spoken boldly in the name of Jesus. So he came and went in their company at Jerusalem, and spoke boldly in the name of the Lord. He preached, besides, to the Jews who talked Greek, and disputed with them, till they set about trying to take his life. As soon as they heard of this, the brethren took him down to Caesarea, and put him on his way to Tarsus. (Acts 9: 23–30)

B

PAUL'S VOCATION

The Lord's call to Paul is imperative, a command: 'Go on thy way: I mean to send thee on a distant errand, to the Gentiles'. The very words that Paul himself uses suggests that we should look back to the calling of the prophet Jeremiah.

'The word of the Lord came to me, and his message was: "I claimed thee for my own before ever I fashioned thee in thy mother's womb; before ever thou camest to the birth, I set thee apart for myself; I have a prophet's errand for thee among the nations".'

Jeremiah raises objections; 'Alas, alas, Lord God, I am but a child that has never learned to speak' (so, too, Paul will write in one of his letters that he is not skilled in the art of talking).

And Yahweh answers Jeremiah: 'A child, sayest thou? Nay, I have a mission for thee to undertake, a message to entrust to thee. Have no human fears; am I not at thy side, to protect thee from harm?' (Jer. 1: 4-8).

Paul is well aware that the mission laid upon him is unequivocal and compelling: 'When I preach the gospel, I take no

They let him down the wall in a hamper (Acts 9: 25). (Monreale Cathedral)

The Walls of Damascus

'I have been everything by turns to everbody' (1 Cor. 9: 22)

credit for that; I act under constraint; it would go hard with me
indeed if I did not preach the gospel' (1 Cor. 9: 16).

St. Paul's missionary method is to go along with his hearers to
the limit that is possible without transgression; he has to tell
them the Good News, and he seeks them out where they are,
makes himself as one of them, tries to think with their minds so
that he may lead them to Christ.

> Thus nobody has any claim on me, and yet I have made my-
> self everybody's slave, to win more souls. With the Jews I lived
> like a Jew, to win the Jews; with those who keep the law, as one
> who keeps the law (though the law had no claim on me), to win
> those who kept the law; with those who are free of the law, like
> one free of the law (not that I disowned all divine law, but it

35

was the law of Christ that bound me), to win those who were free of the law. With the scrupulous, I behave myself like one who is scrupulous, to win the scrupulous. I have been everything by turns to everybody, to bring everybody salvation. All that I do, I do for the sake of the gospel promises, to win myself a share in them. (1 Cor. 9: 19–23)

PAUL'S LETTERS

The first two of St. Paul's letters that we have date from the year 51, about fifteen years after his conversion. He had already established a number of churches, and these two letters were directed to the brethren at Thessalonica.

Paul's letters to the churches were addressed to communities he had himself planted, and were written in view of particular circumstances and to meet particular needs. They therefore express only some of the elements of his thought and faith; at the same time, he is able to draw out of specific problems considerations that have a universal bearing. Generally speaking, he takes it for granted that his correspondents know the fundamentals of the teaching that he gave in person to these communities when he formed them; the letters only complete or fill out

'I act under constraint; it would go hard with me indeed if I did not preach the gospel' (1 Cor. 9: 16). (Palermo)

'The chief message I handed on to you, as it was handed on to me'
1 Cor. 15: 3. (Monreale)

or repeat a basic oral teaching. There is an echo of this initial teaching in certain passages of the Epistles: 'The chief message I handed on to you, as it was handed on to me, was that Christ, as the scriptures had foretold, died for our sins; that he was buried, and then, as the scriptures had foretold, rose again on the third day . . .' (1 Cor. 15: 3–4). He reminds the Galatians that he has set the Crucified Christ before their eyes (Gal. 3: 1). Those things are the fundamental elements of Christian teaching, nourishing milk for those newly born in Christ.

But the writings available do not permit a reconstruction of Paul's theology as a systematic whole. It is in any case simply the Church's theology. Paul had seen the Risen Christ and received the Gospel directly from him; and he also received a 'tradition' from the primitive apostolic community. The mind of Paul, in its turn, exerted an influence on the composition of the written gospels. It follows that it is hardly possible to reconstitute whatever development there was in Paul's thought. Its essence was imparted when Christ manifested himself to him. The great Christological writings of the letters written from prison (Colossians, Ephesians, Philippians) perhaps represent

37

the substance of the teaching he gave to communities during his first missions to them. In any case they are partly a handing on of the truth that Christ revealed to him at that first manifestation.

Accordingly, in the pages that follow, passages from the various letters are used dialectically, grouped so far as possible according to theme, but without taking into account the different dates at which the letters were written.*

These letters are not the production of a leisured life, Paul dictated them at odd moments, in intervals of earning his living and preaching the Gospel. Did he dictate them standing up, or walking to and fro as the words came? More likely, perhaps, he dictated while his hands were busied in tent-making. They have all the marks of oral speech, and the longer ones were interrupted from time to time and then returned to. To write out a letter on papyrus was a long business, and hard work for the scribe; a long one was a matter of several days, which accounts for the disconnectedness and failures of continuity in the Pauline epistles.

Nor must we look for literary airs and graces. Paul was talking to his beloved churches when he was far away from them: they

---

* An introductory work such as this is not the place for technical discussion of how approximate dates and places of the composition of the Epistles can be arrived at. Consult on this *A Catholic Commentary on Holy Scripture* (London, 1953) or the *Bible de Jérusalem* (Paris, 1956; English translation in preparation).

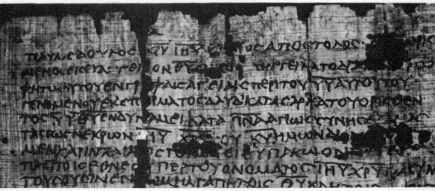

Romans 1: 1–7 in the Oxyrhynchus Papyrus; early 4th century

are love-letters, ardent, solicitous; fatherly, brotherly, even motherly letters. He writes to the Galatians (4: 19): 'My little children, I am in travail over you afresh, until I can see Christ's image formed in you!' These churches that he has brought to birth are his joy, his glory and his crown: 'My brethren, so greatly loved and longed for, all my delight and prize . . .' (Phil. 4: 1); our 'prize to boast of' (1 Thess. 2: 19); 'You are my dearly loved children, and I would bring you to a better mind. Yes, you may have ten thousand schoolmasters in Christ, but not more than one father; it was I that begot you in Jesus Christ, when I preached the gospel to you' (1 Cor. 4: 14–15). In the first letter to the Thessalonians (2: 7–8) he introduces the idea of nursing: 'You found us innocent as babes in your company; no nursing mother ever cherished her children more; in our great longing for you, we desired nothing better than to offer you our own lives, as well as God's gospel, so greatly had we learned to love you.'

The way in which Paul's letters were composed and the circumstances of their dictation account in part for the roughness of their style; sentences are begun and then left in the air, there are sudden changes of perspective, repetitions, an occasional moment of tedium . . .

ESIGN AND PURPOSE OF GOD'S WORK

THE MYSTERY OF CHRIST

St. Paul was called to labour in a work that was begun long before him and will be finished only long after him, when mankind will have reached the age of the fullness of Christ and Christ will be all in all. Paul was, as he says himself, a fellow worker with God in that work to which the Lord called him 'from his mother's womb'.

What, then, is the economy, the 'scheme', of this work whose stages are the creation of the world, the choosing of a holy people, the deliverance of mankind and finally man's adoption to sonship, being called to be joint-heir with the Son who is co-eternal with God? If we are to grasp the significance of St. Paul's life and mind we have to consider—even if only summarily—the nature of this divine work in which he came to take part in his time—a time which put an end to time.

On the road to Damascus Paul met the Risen Christ: he says so himself—he learned everything from Christ in glory. This meeting was the decisive moment of his life. So we have to see what this mystery of Christ is, for it is the key to the mystery of

Initial letter from the 14th century
Psalter of Robert of Ormesby
(Bodleian Library)

God's creation. We must briefly examine the genesis of certain biblical ideas, in order to understand the meaning of the drama in which Paul at his hour—a late hour—came to play a leading part. We must seek to understand the mystery whose unfolding was begun by the prophets of Israel, which was revealed in its fullness in the Word of God when he came among us.

The mystery of Christ is not a doctrine 'thought up' by St. Paul, he did not invent it: the mystery of the eternal Christ was *revealed* to him by Christ himself. Paul is not an 'author', whose biography somebody writes and then goes on to expound his work and ideas. Not at all; Paul's own existence is made a part of the economy of the mystery of Christ, to be its minister and preacher. Paul would have been horrified by the term 'Paulinism' which has been applied to the teaching found in his letters.

Paul's thought, according to himself, is Christ's mind, which has been revealed to him, Paul, and has taught him the breadth and length and depth of God's mystery. He writes to the Corinthians (1 Cor. 1: 11–13): 'The account I have of you, my brethren, . . . is that there are dissensions among you; each of you, I mean, has a cry of his own, I am for Paul, I am for Apollo, I am for Cephas, I am for Christ. What, has Christ been divided up? Was it Paul that was crucified for you? Was it in Paul's name that you were baptized?' Nothing could be more 'un-Pauline' that to see in 'Paulinism' anything else but the mind of Christ and of the Church. Paul's foundation was Christ, he was grafted into Christ, all his life, knowledge and spiritual understanding came to him from Christ. Paul's activity was Christ's activity working in him; Christ was his very being: 'I am alive; or rather, not I; it is Christ that lives in me . . . For me, life means Christ . . .'

If, then, we are to be faithful to Paul's spirit, we must begin by outlining this mystery of God's Anointed One, using principally Paul's own writings. By so doing we shall be able to present his life and mind and activities in the context of his own vision of the world: Paul as he saw himself, in his own time and place, in the economy of creation and salvation.

The revelation of the mystery of God's work draws towards

its close with St. Paul; he was the last to see the Risen Christ, and his synthesis is a final stage of revelation.

The crucial moment at which to study any developing reality is the moment when its evolution is complete. The structure and meaning of an embryonic phenomenon is fully understood only when it is examined at the time of its wholeness as envisaged from the beginning. One cannot see the significance and anatomy of an embryonic substance until one sees the organism come to full growth. This applies also to biblical theology.

The study and elucidation of the meaning of the inspired books of the Old Covenant cannot be effectively undertaken otherwise than from the point of view of the goal that the books themselves anticipate, the end towards which their hope and expectation are always directed. The significance of these inspired books, their purposive direction that makes them prophetical, is finally Christ, who is Fulfilment. When the Scriptures are read for their inner meaning, Christ can never be, as it were, put in parenthesis. That is what Paul said with reference to those Jews who had not reached any understanding of the mystery of Christ: 'To this day the reading of the old law is muffled with the same veil; no revelation tells them that it has been abrogated in Christ. To this day, I say, when the law of Moses is read out, a veil hangs over their hearts [*i.e.*, their understanding]. There must be a turning to the Lord first, and then the veil will be taken away. The Spirit we have been speaking of is the Lord: and where the Lord's Spirit is, there is freedom' (2 Cor. 3: 14–17).

We will endeavour in this part to give the elements of a synthesis of biblical theology, made from St. Paul's standpoint. Then, in a second part, we will try to show Paul's place in the decisive moment of the history of God's people, and how his actual, concrete experience, his whole life, is a source of theological truth for him and for us.

What is the 'gospel which reveals the mystery, hidden from us through countless ages, but now made plain, through what the prophets have written; now published, at the eternal God's command, to all the nations, so as to win the homage of their faith'? (Rom. 16: 25–26); 'The secret that had been hidden

42

from all the ages and generations of the past; now, he has revealed it to his saints, wishing to make known the manifold splendour of this secret among the Gentiles—Christ among you, your hope of glory . . .' Paul writes to the Colossians to help them to be 'enriched in every way with fuller understanding, so as to penetrate the secret revealed to us by God the Father, and by Jesus Christ, in whom the whole treasury of wisdom and knowledge is stored up. . . . Take care not to let anyone cheat you with his philosophizings, with empty phantasies drawn from human tradition, from worldly principles; they were never Christ's teaching. In Christ the whole plentitude of Deity is embodied, and dwells in him' (Col. 1: 26, 2: 2–3, 8–9).

Christ between the Church and the
Synagogue (2 Cor. 3: 14).
(Window at Saint-Denis)

You have received the spirit of adoption, which makes us cry out, Abba! Father! Rom. 8: 15. (Chartres)

ADOPTION

What is the meaning of God's work, what is its purpose? It is *adoption*, whereby created man is invited and called to share the life of God, in Christ, with whom we become joint-heirs. 'The spirit you have now received is not, as of old, a spirit of slavery, to govern you by fear; it is the spirit of adoption, which makes us cry out, Abba, Father. The Spirit himself thus assures our spirit, that we are children of God; and if we are his children, then we are his heirs too; heirs of God, sharing the inheritance of Christ; only we must share his sufferings, if we are to share his glory' (Rom. 8: 15–17).

All creation finds its fulfilment in this adoption of man as son of God: its hour has come, as when a woman brings forth her child.

Not that I count these present sufferings as the measure of that glory which is to be revealed in us. If creation is full of expectancy, that is because it is waiting for the sons of God to be made known. Created nature has been condemned to frustration; not for some deliberate fault of its own, but for the sake of him who so condemned it, with a hope to look forward to; namely, that nature in its turn will be set free from the tyranny of corruption, to share in the glorious freedom of God's sons. The whole of nature, as we know, groans in a common travail all the while. And not only do we see that, but we ourselves do the same; we ourselves, although we have already begun to reap our spiritual harvest, groan in our hearts, waiting for that adoption which is the ransoming of our bodies from their slavery. It must be so, since our salvation is founded upon the hope of something. Hope would not be hope at all if its object were in view; how could a man still hope for something which he sees? And if we are hoping for something still unseen, then we need endurance to wait for it.

Only, as before, the Spirit comes to the aid of our weakness; when we do not know what prayer to offer, to pray as we ought, the Spirit himself intercedes for us, with groans beyond all utterance: and God, who can read our hearts, knows well what the Spirit's intent is; for indeed it is according to the mind of God that he makes intercession for the saints. Meanwhile, we are well assured that everything helps to secure the good of those who love God, those whom he has called in fulfilment of his design. All those who from the first were known to him, he has destined from the first to be moulded into the image of his Son, who is thus to become the eldest-born among many brethren. So predestined, he called them; so called, he justified them; so justified, he glorified them. (Rom. 8: 18–30)

Blessed be that God, that Father of our Lord Jesus Christ, who has blessed us, in Christ, with every spiritual blessing, higher than heaven itself. He has chosen us out, in Christ, before the foundation of the world, to be saints, to be blameless in his sight, for love of him; marking us out beforehand (so his will decreed) to be his adopted children through Jesus Christ. Thus he would manifest the splendour of that grace by which he has taken us into his favour in the person of his beloved Son.

It is in him and through his blood that we enjoy redemption, the forgiveness of our sins. So rich is God's grace, that has overflowed upon us in a full stream of wisdom and discernment, to make known to us the hidden purpose of his will. It was his loving design, centred in Christ, to give history its fulfilment by resuming everything in him, all that is in heaven, all that is on earth, summed up in him. In him it was our lot to be called, singled out beforehand to suit his purpose (for it is he who is at work everywhere, carrying out the designs of his will); we were to manifest his glory, we who were the first to set our hope in Christ; in him you too were called, when you listened to the preaching of the truth, that gospel which is your salvation. In him you too learned to believe, and had the seal set on your faith by the promised gift of the Holy Spirit. (Eph. 1: 3–13)

So may he who is the God of our Lord Jesus Christ, the Father to whom glory belongs, grant you a spirit of wisdom and insight, to give you fuller knowledge of himself. May your inward eye be enlightened, so that you may understand to what hopes he has called you, how rich in glory is that inheritance of his found among the saints, what surpassing virtue there is in his dealings with us, who believe. Measure it by that mighty exercise of power which he shewed when he raised Christ from the dead, and bade him sit on his right hand above the heavens, high above all princedoms and powers and virtues and dominations, and every name that is known, not in this world only, but in the world to come. He has put everything under his dominion, and made him the head to which the whole Church is joined, so that the Church is his body, the completion of him who everywhere and in all things is complete. (Eph. 1: 17–23)

It [this secret of Christ's] was never made known to any human being in past ages, as it has now been revealed by the Spirit to his holy apostles and prophets, and it is this: that through the gospel preaching the Gentiles are to win the same inheritance, to be made part of the same body, to share the same divine promise, in Christ Jesus. With what grace God gives me (and he gives it in all the effectiveness of his power), I am a minister of that gospel; on me, least as I am of all the saints, he has bestowed this privilege, of making known to the Gentiles the unfathomable riches of Christ, of publishing to the world the plan of this mystery, kept hidden from the beginning of time in the all-creating mind of God. The principalities and powers of heaven are to see, now, made manifest in the Church, the subtely of God's wisdom; such is his eternal purpose, centred in Christ Jesus our Lord. . . . (Eph. 3: 5–11)

To express the 'plan' of God's work, its effective means and their carrying out, Paul uses the Greek word *oikonomia*. This Pauline term is here translated 'economy', a word used in thermodynamics to designate the functional arrangement and power-yield of a thermal mechanism; it is also used in biology, for the physiology of an organism, the arrangement that enables it to move, to energize, to renew itself—in a word, to live. The exact sense of 'economy' in St. Paul's theology will become clearer as we go along.

'With what grace God gives me . . . I am a minister of that gospel' (Eph. 3: 7). (Moissac)

In him all created things took their being,
heavenly and earthly, visible and invisible
Col. 1: 16. (Chartres)

THE DESIGN OF CREATION

We must examine the design and economy of this work of God. The world was created by and through his Word: 'It is faith that lets us understand how the worlds were fashioned by God's word; how it was from things unseen that the things we see took their origin' (Heb. 11: 3). Faith is a supernatural understanding conferred by the Spirit, and it attains to the very principle of being, a principle that is hidden and unseen—the Word of God. This Word is Somebody. 'In old days, God spoke to our fathers in many ways and by many means, through the prophets; now at last in these times he has spoken to us with a Son to speak for him; a Son, whom he has appointed to inherit all things, just as it was through him that he created this world of time' (Heb. 1: 1–2).

The pre-existing Word of God is the Son, Christ; 'He is the true likeness of the God we cannot see; his is that first birth which precedes every act of creation. Yes, in him all created things took their being, heavenly and earthly, visible and invisible . . . They were all created through him and in him; he takes precedency of all, and in him all things subsist. He too is that head whose body is the Church; it begins with him, since his was the first birth out of death; thus in every way the primacy was to become his. It was God's good pleasure to let all completeness dwell in him, and through him to win back all things . . . into union with himself, making peace with them through his blood, shed on the cross' (Col. 1: 15–20). Christ is the principle and end of all creation; he is *alpha* and *omega*, the first and the last; he is the root and the head of God's work. Everything comes from him, everything has been brought into being by him, everything is directed towards him, everything finds its fulfilment in him. 'At the beginning of time the Word already was; and God had the Word abiding with him, and the Word was God. He abode, at the beginning of time, with God. It was through him that all things came into being, and without him came nothing that has come to be. In him there was life, and that life was the light of men . . .' (John 1: 1–4).

Looking back, we nowadays know something of the course of creation since its first beginning. Up to a point we are able to see its meaning, its direction and object. We know from positive investigation that creation began with matter, the constitution of a physical universe, cosmogenesis; then, at the second stage, came life, a flowering of animal species, of well-determined character: in the course of time the tree of life was set towards living forms that were ever more mobile, free and conscious.

49

The goal of this cosmic and biological process was man; and human history took over from biological evolution, in the same way that evolution had taken over from cosmogenesis.

But the work of creation does not come to an end with man's appearance on the scene: instead, it passes from the plane of solitary creation by God to a process of creation in association with a being itself created, who becomes a participant in creation. Man is created, but he co-operates in his own genesis, he has to consent to his own fulfilment. He is invited and called to become a god, able to share in the life of God: 'Gods you are, I myself have declared it; favoured children, every one of you, of the most High' (Ps. 81 [82]: 6), and Christ in turn takes up that declaration: ' Is it not written in your law, I have said, " You are gods . . . and we know that the words of scripture have binding force "?' (John 10: 34–35).

From the moment that man is called to co-operate in his own destiny, a supernatural destiny, a great change comes over the work of creation: it leaves the 'natural' order for one of participation in God's life, a 'supernatural' order. God weds his creation, in the person of his beloved people, Israel. He freely joins with himself the being whom he has created, who as freely consents to the union. The meaning of creation is precisely this personal union.

Man as he is, in his actual state, is not complete. He is not complete biologically, psychologically or socially; more radically, he is not complete in that he has not reached the definitive constitution of his existence, the fullness of the call which he has to accept, namely, to become like to God his creator, in order that he may share in his life. 'God said, "Let us make man, wearing our own image, and likeness"' (Gen. 1: 26). We have only to look within ourselves and around us to see that mankind is still far from being in the image and likeness of God.

The creation of a human race able to resemble God, the formation of a people of God: thus is ushered in a further stage of God's creation, a new, supernatural process, a sacred history. From the beginning of cosmic matter and the making of the galaxies to the constitution of a holy people, from one to the other,

God's creative deed is unfolded with one single object (though according to distinct stages and patterns, passing from a natural to a supernatural order): and that one aim is the sharing by the created being of the life of the Creator, in Christ, through the Holy Spirit. It is impossible to understand St. Paul unless we look at things from this cosmic standpoint.

THE OLD AND THE NEW MAN

St. Paul shows us the pattern of the economy of man's creation in a chapter of the first letter to the Corinthians that is devoted to the resurrection. 'Mankind begins with the Adam who

51

'*Be clothed in the new self, which is created in God's image, justified and sanctified through the truth*' *Eph.* 4: 24. (*Autun*)

became, as Scripture tells us [in Gen. 2: 7], a living soul; it is fulfilled in the Adam who has become a life-giving spirit. It was not the principle of spiritual life that came first; natural ['psychic'] life came first, then spiritual life; the man who came first came from earth, fashioned of dust, the man who came afterwards came from heaven' (1 Cor. 15: 45–47).

In this passage Paul distinguishes between the natural, 'psychic', order and the spiritual order. The book of Genesis tells us that the first man was created 'a living soul'; but according to the Hebrew Bible animals also are living souls. The whole animal kingdom, biologically considered, is in the Bible called 'the flesh'; the Hebrew uses the expressions 'every living soul' and 'all flesh' as equivalents, meaning the animal biological order. 'All flesh' may be the aggregate of living creatures, men as well as beasts (cf. Gen. 6: 13, 17; 7: 15; Ps. 136: 25); or more particularly, the aggregate of men alone (cf. Gen. 6: 12; Isa. 40: 6; Jer. 12: 12, 25: 31; Zech. 2: 13). The flesh, then, in the biblical sense, is this biological order, quickened, living and conscious. If, as many biologists think, consciousness is co-extensive with life, then the biblical view is very 'modern': biology is also psychology.

To this biological-psychological order, Paul opposes that which he calls spiritual (*pneumatikon*). This spiritual order is 'from Heaven', that is, supernatural, and, he says, it comes 'afterward' in the design of God's creation: it is a completing of man, accorded in order that he may fulfil his supernatural destiny. The first man is 'fashioned of dust', for he comes from the earth. In Hebrew the word *adam* simply means man, in the specific sense. This first mankind is animal, coming from the animal world. The second mankind, the second Adam, will be of Heaven, by a transformation that is God's work through Christ and in the Spirit.

So two stages are necessary for the completion of man and to enable him to attain the fullness of his destiny, in accordance with the prophetical word of Genesis, which promises that he shall be created in the image and likeness of God. The first stage carries the natural creation forward through cosmogenesis and biogenesis. The second stage marks a definitive advance, from a natural to the supernatural order: it is the creation of a holy, spiritual mankind, indwelt by God's holy Spirit, to share with Christ in the trinitarian life of God. The whole creation has been brought about in Christ; it is carried on in Christ, through the making supernatural of mankind and the formation of a spiritual humanity; it will be consummated in Christ, when his mystical Body reaches 'the measure of his stature', its fullness, when God shall be all in all. This will not happen till the final resurrection, when Christ will give back the kingdom into his Father's hands.

Man, then, must be *born again*; St. John's gospel says so explicitly: 'Jesus answered "... a man cannot see the kingdom of God without being born anew." "Why," Nicodemus asked him, "how is it possible that a man should be born when he is already old? Can he enter a second time into his mother's womb, and so come to birth?" Jesus answered, "Believe me, no man can enter into the kingdom of God unless birth comes to him from water, and from the Holy Spirit. What is born by natural birth is a thing of nature, what is born by spiritual birth is a thing of spirit"' (John 3: 3–6).

That is just what St. Paul says. Man, who has been created a biological, psychological being, 'flesh', has to be transformed, in Christ and by the Spirit of God, into a spiritual being, a creature fit for God. 'When a man becomes a new creature in Christ, his old life has disappeared, everything has become new about

'This mortal nature must be clothed with immortality'
1 *Cor.* 15: 53. (*Autun*)

'What we have received is no spirit of worldly wisdom; it is the Spirit that comes from God' 1 Cor. 2: 12. (Palermo)

him' (2 Cor. 5: 17). Christ has come to make a new man (Eph. 2: 15), and it is our business to co-operate in this change, stripping off the old man and becoming the new, 'You must be quit, now, of the old self . . ., the self that wasted its aim on false dreams . . . you must be clothed in the new self, which is created in God's image, justified and sanctified through the truth' (Eph. 4: 22–24); 'You must be quit of the old self, and the habits that went with it; you must be clothed in the new self, that is being refitted all the time for closer knowledge, so that the image of the God who created it is its pattern' (Col. 3: 9–10).

It is very necessary to bear in mind the twofold implication of the notion of 'flesh' in the Bible, and especially in St. Paul. In biblical terminology, as we have seen, flesh is first of all the created biological, psychological ('quickened'), living order, more particularly mankind, and the term then has no depreciatory connotation at all. The 'all flesh' of the Bible may be translated simply as 'all living creatures' or, in the restricted sense, 'men'; for example, in Isaiah (40: 5): 'The glory of the Lord shall be revealed, and all flesh shall see', and in Jeremiah (32: 27): 'I am the Lord, the God of all flesh'.* It must be carefully noticed that in the Bible 'the flesh' does *not* signify a *part* of the human whole, as it does in a dualist anthropology that speaks of 'body' and 'soul'. The biblical notion of flesh is not equivalent to the Western notion of 'body'. We repeat, for the Bible flesh is mankind, man *in his wholeness*, or the animal kingdom including the living, quickened, conscious human world.

But mankind has a will of its own, choice of what it does and how it does it, freedom of thought and action, responsibility for its destiny. As things are, it is as it was in the days of Noah: the earth was corrupt and full of evil-doing, God saw that all flesh had become corrupted (Gen. 6: 11–12). And so, beyond its neutral sense of living creature, the Bible gives to flesh a further, reproachful, sense, of that creature perverted and in rebellion; the Old Testament came to use it for man's perverse will, his weakness and sinfulness. But here again we must beware of confusing the biblical conception with the quite different idea that the Manichean and various gnostic heresies brought into the Western world; flesh means one thing in the Bible and another thing in the gnostic metaphysic. For Manes and Marcion the flesh is evil, it is the body in which the soul is shut up as in a filthy prison. Once again, in the Bible the flesh does not signify a *part* of man; rather, man *is* flesh. While for the dualist

---

* These are from the Douay version. In his translation of these texts, Mgr Knox indicates the meaning by rendering 'flesh' as 'all mankind' and 'all that lives'.

Manichean a man is substantially a soul, imprisoned in a body.

Unless these distinctions are carefully borne in mind, the Pauline passages we are going to quote will be wholly misunderstood. We have to be aware of the heterogeneous origins of our Western heritage of ideas and terms, otherwise apparent analogies of vocabulary will betray us into making identifications where there is in fact complete difference. Here what happened was that gnostic Christians falsified the meaning of Paul's terms, and interpreted the biblical notion of flesh from the standpoint of a metaphysic of Platonic type. So far from signifying a *thing* (the body), the word flesh in the Bible connotes rather a certain *state of mind*, a *wilfulness*, found in mankind following its own devices and desires. The flesh is the human being in so far as he opposes God, the 'old self' not yet renewed by supernatural life —the spirit.

In St. Paul and St. John the idea of flesh carries the same ambivalence as the idea of *kosmos*, 'world'. In one meaning for John, the world is God's creation, which is good, and more particularly mankind, the human world: 'God so loved the world, that he gave up his only begotten Son, so that those who believe in him may not perish, but have eternal life' (John 3: 16). Sometimes, on the other hand, the world signifies, like the flesh, the world of men whose will is in oppposition to God's will. In this human world man's sin is, as it were, crystallized, objectified, in institutions, forms, manners and customs, ways, ready-made judgements—the whole collective mentality that Heidegger calls 'what "they" think', what 'everybody' says: gossip and inquisitiveness, bad faith, 'looking after Number One', the tyranny of certain values that are worthless in God's sight. All this can be what St. John calls 'the sin of the world' (John 1: 29); it is simply what the Old Testament calls the sin of the children of men, of human kind: the world can find no room for the truth-giving Spirit (John 14: 17). 'If you belonged to the world, the world would know you for its own and love you; it is because you do not belong to the world, because I have singled you out from the midst of the world, that the world hates you' (John 15: 19). Clearly there is no question here of the

56

physical cosmos, but of that world of men which bears so heavily on each one of us. That world, too, has its own wisdom: 'This world's wisdom,' writes St. Paul, 'with God, is but folly' (1 Cor. 3:19); 'The world, with all its wisdom, could not find its way to God' (1 Cor. 1: 21); 'And what we have received is no spirit of worldly wisdom; it is the Spirit that comes from God . . . which we make known, not in such words as human wisdom teaches, but in words taught us by the Spirit . . .' (1 Cor. 2: 12).

In all these texts 'the world' has an existential, not a cosmological, significance, just as the use of 'the flesh' is existential and not anthropological. Following on those of Pascal and Kierkegaard, the analyses of Heidegger are valuable for drawing out the content of these biblical ideas.

This expression 'world' is another New Testament term that the gnostics perverted, transposing the biblical idea into a metaphysic of the Fall: according to them, pre-existing souls have fallen into the evil world, into the matter that holds them in thrall. This corruption of the meaning of words as used by St. Paul still exists in a measure, and it is very difficult to get people to think of them in the original sense.

In a sentence, then: In the passages that follow, St. Paul does not say that 'the body is evil' (that is the Manichean view), but that 'in its actuality, mankind tends towards sinfulness' and resists God's call—a quite different thing.

Man resists God's will, and consequently there is opposition between the spirit of the world and the Spirit of God. When the Spirit of God comes to dwell in us and seeks to transform us into spiritual beings, godly beings, it meets with resistance from the 'old self's' spirit of opposition. Hence our state of chronic indecision: we can either act according to the old self in us and refuse God's proffered renewal, or we can act according to his Spirit, calling us to the freedom of the divine life. It is this that Paul describes as the opposition between 'flesh' and 'spirit'.*

---

* In Mgr Knox's translation, 'flesh' in this sense is commonly rendered by 'nature' or 'corrupt nature'.

Let me say this; learn to live and move in the spirit; then there is no danger of your giving way to the impulses of corrupt nature. The impulses of nature and the impulses of the spirit are at war with one another; either is clean contrary to the other, and that is why you cannot do all that your will approves. It is by letting the spirit lead you that you free yourselves from the yoke of the law.

It is easy to see what effects proceed from corrupt nature; they are such things as adultery, impurity, incontinence, luxury, idolatry, witchcraft, feuds, quarrels, jealousies, outbursts of anger, rivalries, dissensions, factions, spite, murder, drunkenness, and debauchery. I warn you, as I have warned you before, that those who live in such a way will not inherit God's kingdom.

Whereas the spirit yields a harvest of love, joy, peace, patience, kindness, generosity, . . . faith, courtesy, temperateness . . . No law can touch lives such as these; those who belong to Christ have crucified nature, with all its passions, all its impulses. (Gal. 5: 16–24)

As St. Augustine remarks in *The City of God* (xiv, 2), the works, the deeds, of the flesh are not solely those actions that we associate with the body, debauchery and the like; they are also psychological actions and behaviour, such as hate, jealousy, anger, superstition, separatism, which come under the heading of psychology while having a biological and bodily substratum. The spiritual is that which is not psychoanalysable: it does not depend on the biological, psychological, human order, but on the supernatural order, that is, on the life of God. For Paul, carnal, fleshly, signifies human; to live 'according to the flesh' means to live merely as a human being. He writes to the Corinthians (1 Cor. 3: 1–3): 'When I preached to you, I had to approach you as men with natural, not with spiritual thoughts. You were little children in Christ's nursery, and I gave you milk, not meat; you were not strong enough for it. You are not strong enough for it even now; nature still lives in you. Do not these rivalries, these dissensions among you shew that nature is still alive, that you are guided by human standards?'

To live according to the flesh and the world is to live 'marked out for death', *eis thanaton*, 'for the reward of those things is death . . . if you live a life of nature you are marked out for death'. Living carnally is to lead the existence of a human being who has not been restored by life according to Christ's Spirit, a life-giving spirit of renewal: 'Those who follow the leading of God's Spirit are all God's sons' (Rom. 6: 16, 21; 8: 13, 14). Pascal's analyses of the state of man without God, and those of Heidegger and his followers, illustrate this negation of Christian existence, the lack which supernatural life comes to fill. There is, writes Paul, a 'supernatural remorse' that 'leads to an abiding and salutary change of heart, whereas the world's remorse leads to death' (2 Cor. 7: 10). The sorrow of the world is the hopelessness of existence 'according to the flesh', existence of a simply human sort, the *Geworfenheit*, 'being-thrown-into-the-world'. Heidegger's universe is a Christian universe with the hope of salvation taken away.

> . . . so that we should be fully quit of the law's claim, we, who follow the ways of the spirit, not the ways of flesh and blood. To live the life of nature is to think the thoughts of nature; to live the life of the spirit is to think the thoughts of the spirit; and natural wisdom brings only death, whereas the wisdom of the spirit brings life and peace. That is because natural wisdom is at enmity with God, not submitting itself to his law; it is impossible that it should. Those who live the life of nature cannot be acceptable to God; but you live the life of the spirit, not the life of nature; that is, if the Spirit of God dwells in you. A man cannot belong to Christ unless he has the Spirit of Christ. But if Christ lives in you, then although the body be a dead thing in virtue of our guilt, the spirit is a living thing, by virtue of our justification. And if the spirit of him who raised up Jesus from the dead dwells in you, he who raised up Jesus Christ from the dead will give life to your perishable bodies too, for the sake of his Spirit who dwells in you. (Rom. 8: 4–11)

CREATION FULFILLED: THE RESURRECTION

Creation will not be completed till the day of resurrection, which will usher in the messianic kingdom and a new 'time'. what the Bible calls the time or the world to come, *olam ha*

bah. We are living in a time that is provisional—this present time, *olam ha ze*, 'the time of this world'—the time of still incomplete creation, while the time or world to come is eternal.

With regard to the resurrection of men, St. Paul's starting-

---

* In the New Testament the word *olam* is rendered by the Greek *aion*, which is translated into Latin as *saeculum* and into English generally by 'world' or 'time'.

point is the *fact* of the resurrection of Christ: 'He was seen by Cephas, then by the eleven apostles, and afterwards by more than five hundred of the brethren at once, most of whom are alive at this day, though some have gone to their rest. Then he was seen by James, then by all the apostles; and last of all, I too saw him . . .' (1 Cor. 15: 5–8). Resurrection from the dead is possible, because Christ rose again: Paul's argument rests on that fact, to testify to the truth of which its witnesses will undergo torments. How will the resurrection come about?

If what we preach about Christ, then, is that he rose from the dead, how is it that some of you say the dead do not rise again? If the dead do not rise, then Christ has not risen either; and if Christ has not risen, then our preaching is groundless, and your faith, too, is groundless. Worse still, we are convicted of giving false testimony about God; we bore God witness that he had raised Christ up from the dead, and he has not raised him up, if it is true that the dead do not rise again. If the dead, I say, do not rise, then Christ has not risen either; and if Christ has not risen, all your faith is delusion; you are back in your sins. It follows, too, that those who have gone to their rest in Christ have been lost. If the hope we have learned to repose in Christ belongs to this world only, then we are unhappy beyond all other men. But no, Christ has risen from the dead, the first-fruits of all those who have fallen asleep; a man had brought us death, and a man should bring us resurrection from the dead; just as all have died with Adam, so with Christ all will be brought to life. But each must rise in his own rank; Christ is the first-fruits, and after him follow those who belong to him, those who have put their trust in his return. Full completion comes after that, when he places his kingship in the hands of God, his Father, having first dispossessed every other sort of rule, authority, and power; his reign, as we know, must continue until he has put all his enemies under his feet, and the last of those enemies to be dispossessed is death. God has put all things in subjection under his feet; that is, all things have been made subject to him, except indeed that power which made them his subjects. And when that subjection is complete, then the Son himself will become subject to the power which made all things his subjects, so that God may be all in all . . .

But perhaps someone will ask, How can the dead rise up? What kind of body will they be wearing when they appear? Poor fool, when thou sowest seed in the ground, it must die before it can be brought to life; and what thou sowest is not the full body that is one day to be, it is only bare grain, of wheat, it may be, or some other crop; it is for God to embody it according to his will, each grain in the body that belongs to it. Nature is not all one; men have one nature, the beasts another, the birds another, the fishes another; so, too, there are bodies that belong to earth and bodies that belong to heaven; and heavenly bodies have one kind of beauty, earthly bodies another. The sun has its own beauty, the moon has hers, the stars have theirs, one star even differs from another in its beauty.

So it is with the resurrection of the dead. What is sown corruptible, rises incorruptible; what is sown unhonoured, rises in glory; what is sown in weakness is raised in power; what is sown a natural body, rises a spiritual body. If there is such a·thing as a natural body, there must be a spiritual body too. Mankind begins with the Adam who became, as Scripture tells us, a living soul: it is fulfilled in the Adam who has become a life-giving spirit. It was not the principle of spiritual life that came first; natural life came first, then spiritual life; the man who came first came from earth, fashioned of dust, the man who came afterwards came from heaven, and his fashion is heavenly. The nature of that earth-born man is shared by his earthly sons, the nature of the heaven-born man, by his heavenly sons; and it remains for us, who once bore the stamp of earth, to bear the stamp of heaven. What I mean, brethren, is this; the kingdom of God cannot be enjoyed by flesh and blood; the principle of corruption cannot share a life which is incorruptible.

Here is a secret I will make known to you; we shall all rise again, but not all of us will undergo the change I speak of.* It will happen in a moment, in the twinkling of an eye, when the last trumpet sounds; the trumpet will sound, and the dead will rise again, free from corruption, and we shall find ourselves changed; this corruptible nature of ours must be clothed with incorruptible life, this mortal nature with immortality. Then,

* Mgr Knox adds a footnote here which says that a better reading is: 'We shall not all fall asleep, but we shall all be changed.'

when this mortal nature wears its immortality, the saying of scripture will come true, Death is swallowed up in victory. Where then, death, is thy victory; where, death, is thy sting? (1 Cor. 15: 12–28, 35–55).

Christ's resurrection is a pattern of what our own will be. When he rose again and appeared to his disciples, his body was no longer like that which we know; he appeared and vanished without reference to the 'laws' of the world with which we are familiar—he entered a house whose door was shut (John 20: 19). The Lord himself tells us that at the resurrection men will be like angels: they will not marry nor will they eat, for there will be no kind to be carried on and no organism to be nourished; the resurrected body will have no organs. Obviously it is impossible for us to imagine what a 'glorified body' will be like. The resurrection is not a repetition of what went before, the re-establishment of the order of things that we know: it is a transformation, a renewal, a creation. To start off with, the physical, biological world is certainly not constituted and built to last to all eternity, any more than it is constituted to have existed from all eternity. Contrary to what St. Thomas Aquinas said (following the Arab philosophers), we can see that the world of our experience cannot be without beginning: it has an age, it dates from yesterday. In the same way, it is frail and wasting, like ourselves, it is directed to an end, and it will end, tomorrow. God's creation is devised today, in this moment that we call time: 'This day have I begotten thee'.

The physical universe can no more attain to eternity than can existing living bodies; like everything else, it will reach its fulfilment by being transformed, in a way that we cannot picture to ourselves. 'See where I create new heavens and a new earth' (Isa. 65: 17. Cf. 66: 22, and Apoc. [Rev.] 21: 1); 'Those heavens shall vanish like smoke, that earth be fretted away like a garment, and all who dwell on it share the same destruction' (Isa. 51: 6); 'It was thou, Lord, that didst lay the foundations of earth when time began, it was thy hand that built the heavens. They will perish, but thou wilt remain; they will all be like a cloak that grows threadbare, and thou wilt lay them aside like a garment;

'Yahweh said unto Abraham, I will make a great people of thee'
Gen. 12:2. (*Greek manuscript of sixth century*)

and exchange them for new ' (Ps. 101: 26–27 [102: 25–26]). The resurrection, then, will be a true creation, the last stage of creation, its completion, which Paul calls the *pleroma*, the fullness, when Christ will ' form this humbled body of ours anew, moulding it into the image of his glorified body ' (Phil. 3: 21).

THE BEGINNINGS OF GOD'S PEOPLE

When, with the genesis of Israel, God constituted a holy people, his creative activity reached a new and final stage: the crowning of his work by the formation of a people called to share in the Creator's life, the people that is the Lord's bride, his beloved: 'With unchanging love I love thee . . . Israel, poor homeless maid' (Jer. 31: 3). Israel is not a people like other peoples: 'Never think I will allow you to worship wood and stone like other races of men, your neighbours' (Ezek. 20: 32). She is not simply one of the peoples of the earth: she is the beginning, the seed, of a new man, of man in the image and likeness of God, called to have a part in his personal life. Israel is not simply a new kind of nation—rather a new kind of humanity appears in her: for Israel is the beginning of the making super-natural of mankind, that radical transformation which is to make man capable and worthy of divine adoption. Israel is already the Church, the Lord's bride, the mystical Body of Christ.

With the coming of Israel, God's creative activity brings about a passing from the natural to the supernatural order: God's presence in his work, indwelling in his people. It is this coming of God, to establish personal relations between himself and man whom he created, that is called 'the supernatural'. It is there-fore necessary to distinguish between God's creation and his presence in, his gift of himself to, what he has created. This passing from created nature to the supernatural, this communica-tion between the creature and his Creator, is a final stage in the work of charity. 'Listen, then, to my voice, and keep your covenant with me; and I, to whom all the earth belongs, will single you out among its peoples to be my own. You shall serve me as a royal priesthood, as a consecrated nation' (Exod. 19: 5–6).

In order to constitute this holy people, this sanctified and re-newed humanity, God chose Abraham and brought him out of Ur in Chaldea. 'The Lord said to Abram, "Leave thy country behind thee, thy kinsfolk, and thy father's home, and come away into a land I will shew thee. Then I will make a great people of thee; I will bless thee, and make thy name renowned, a name of benediction; those who bless thee, I will bless, those who curse thee, I will curse, and in thee all the races of the world shall find a blessing"' (Gen. 12: 1–3). All the people of the earth were to be transformed in Abraham and in his seed, the nation that was to be like a supernatural leaven in the human dough.

Such an initial setting apart was called for if there was to be a radically new people; a certain state of isolation was needful for the gestation and building up of a renewed mankind. Abraham's exile was the first act of this gestation. 'I, the Lord your God, have set you apart among all the nations of the world . . . to belong

C

to me' (Lev. 20: 24, 26). Remember man's state in the civilizations of the ancient East: the cruelty, the corruption, the sacrifice of children to idols, ritual prostitution, slavery, man exploited and oppressed by man. You will say, 'Yes, and it is still the same. Children are still sacrificed to idols, no different but in their names. Children are burnt alive in myriads before the new Molochs and Baals, the masters of this world.' It is true: and that is why the requirement of exile is continuous and permanent for God's people; like Israel, the Church is not of this world, she does not submit to its masters, its kings and princes, or its gods.

'It is not for you to live by the customs of that Egyptian land in which you once dwelt, or to imitate the men of Chanaan, the new home I am giving you, and follow their observances. It is my decrees you will execute, my commands you will obey, following them closely; am I not the Lord your God?' (Lev. 18: 3–4). 'It is not for you to imitate the practices of the nations I am driving out to make room for you. Was it not these very practices that made me their enemy?' (Lev. 20: 23). Israel must be *separated* in order that she may live: 'Here is a people destined to dwell apart, not counted among the muster-roll of the nations' (Num. 23: 9).

The requirement of holiness was the primary element in the constitution of Israel, the *Law* of Moses was her mould. She was born in God's call and promise to Abraham, but it was the Law of Moses that was her pedagogue. It was this that distinguished her among all the other peoples, the Law, the totality of God's commandments, that kept her from the corruptions of her neighbours: it was both her backbone and her bulwark. Without the Law there would have been no Israel, because like other nations she would have gone after false gods and befouled herself with wickedness and criminality; without the Law she would have been an incomplete organism, not capable of independent existence. The beginning of Israel was in the first place the remaking of a healthy human kind, a regeneration, a redemption.

The Law of Moses was not only a discipline for behaviour, a

life-giving and cleansing ascesis, a wall of protection: it was also instruction. Israel was formed through knowledge; the Torah instructed her in conduct and in mind simultaneously: she was above all a people whom God prepared to know himself. 'Jacob needs no soothsayer, Israel no divination; time will reveal the marvellous things God does for them' (Num. 23: 23); 'It is in Juda God makes himself known' (Ps. 75 [76]: 1). Men would have been unable to receive this knowledge of God had he not prepared them for it, and instruction and discipline through the Law was this preparation, by renewal and deliverance. 'The Lord's commands shall go out from Sion, his word from Jerusalem' (Isa. 2: 3). This instruction and this word were to spread to the uttermost parts of the earth, so that Christ would be able to say, 'Salvation is to come from the Jews' (John 4: 22).

The drama of Israel belongs to her very being; it follows from the seeming contradictions, but really complementaries, inherent in her position. Israel was made a people apart from other peoples, in her nature, her ways of living and thinking, her social, juridical and ethical life. She was an exception, withdrawn, distinct as a people from all other peoples. And yet she was also, and in the first place, the seed of a new humanity, called to transform the whole of mankind. As a people, Israel had to be protected from the influence of the heathendom all around her by the hedge of the Mosaic Law, which kept her to that which she had to be—for only if she remained the exceptional people, the supernatural leaven, the world's salt, could Israel play her predestined part and fulfil her vocation. But that vocation was precisely to transform *all* mankind, and so she had to be open to the other essential aspect of her calling—universality. Should Israel shut herself up in her own exceptionalness, she would not accomplish her destiny of being the firstfruits of the mankind to come.

So two sins, two kinds of unfaithfulness, were possible. Israel could be dissolved in the heathenry that surrounded her; she could betray herself by forsaking the holiness that had to specify her and following gentile ways, idolatry and every other wickedness. By so doing she would betray her vocation and her essence by losing that essence itself: if the salt has lost its savour, wherewith shall it be salted? Alternatively, Israel could be faithless to God's call by turning in on herself, wrapping herself in the complacency of her own righteousness, instead of cultivating the universality that was part of her nature and going out to transform the world, transfiguring man in God.

In fact, Israel was guilty of both these betrayals from time to time throughout her history.

From the time that she entered into the Promised Land, Israel was tempted by her neighbour's ways, by idolatrous cults, cruel observances, bloodthirsty sacrifices, ritual prostitution: she wrought wickedness as the gentiles did. She was faithless to her covenant with the God of Abraham. And accordingly God raised up enemies against her, who persecuted her as God had declared through the prophets, morning after morning, by day and by night, says Isaiah. But Israel did not want to listen to the voice of her God. She was not, in herself, a worse or a better people than any other. It was her humanness that caused her to resist transformation and to be deaf to God's appeal for holy living. We can see that from the fact that the same infidelity still goes on today, among Christians.

The second form of betrayal is the opposite of the first: attachment to the Law at the expense of universality. In both cases Israel tried to be a people like the others, but in different ways. In the first, it was by adopting gentile manners and customs, exactly as God had told her not to do; in the second, she made herself a self-sufficient people, forgetting that she was not simply a people but the beginning of a new mankind, and therefore was not merely one among other nations.

Israel's first failure was continually being denounced by the prophets; her second was characteristic of the crisis which marked the birth of the Christian Church outside of Israel. The Church is Israel, and she knows it. But she is Israel open to all people who seek to know the living God. In order to carry out her vocation as Israel, to be the heir of the promise made to Abraham, 'all the nations of the earth shall be blessed in thee', the Church had to withdraw from Israel as a people.

At the same time as it experienced transforming and spiritual-izing grace, mankind, in the person of Israel, experienced sin, precisely because it opposed and resisted grace. Sin was known only because of the Law. It existed before the Law, from man-kind's very beginning, but it was not known for what it is: it was the Law that brought that knowledge.

Does this mean that law and guilt are the same thing? God forbid we should say that. But it was only the law that gave me my knowledge of sin; I should not even have known concupis-cence for what it is, if the law had not told me, Thou shalt not covet. But the sense of sin, with the law's ban for its foothold, produced in me every sort of concupiscence. Without the law, the sense of sin is a dead thing. At first, without the law, I was alive; then, when the law came with its ban, the sense of sin found new life, and with that, I died. The ban, which was meant to bring life, proved death to me; the sense of sin, with the law's ban for its foothold, caught me unawares, and by that means killed me. The law, to be sure, is something holy; the ban is holy, and right, and good. A good thing, and did it prove death to me? God forbid we should say that. No, it was sin that produced death in me, using this good thing to make itself appear as sin indeed, sin made more sinful than ever by the ban imposed on it. (Rom. 7: 7–13)

By making people conscious of the existence of sin and prompt-ing recognition that it is evil, the Law enabled them to react against it.

The law, as we know, is something spiritual; I am a thing of flesh and blood, sold into the slavery of sin. My own actions bewilder me; what I do is not what I wish to do, but something which I hate. Why then, if what I do is something I have no wish to do, I thereby admit that the law is worthy of all honour; meanwhile, my action does not come from me, but from the sinful principle that dwells in me. Of this I am certain, that no principle of good dwells in me, that is, in my natural self; praiseworthy intentions are always ready to hand, but I cannot find my way to the performance of them; it is not the good my will prefers, but the evil my will disapproves, that I find myself doing. And if what I do is something I have not the will to do, it cannot be I that bring it about, it must be the sinful principle

Israel is freed from Egypt
(Greek manuscript of sixth century)

that dwells in me. This, then, is what I find about the law, that evil is close at my side, when my will is to do what is praiseworthy. Inwardly, I applaud God's disposition, but I observe another disposition in my lower self, which raises war against the disposition of my conscience, and so I am handed over as a captive to that disposition towards sin which my lower self contains. (Rom. 7: 14-23)

CAPTIVITY AND THE HOPE OF FREEDOM

During the course of her history, Israel experienced captivity (firstly in Egypt), oppression, servitude and dereliction. But God in his power brought her out of the house of bondage. He *delivered* Israel, his beloved people, from the oppressive hand of the Egyptians. He *ransomed* enslaved Israel just as, in the days of old, a slave was freed by ransom. He *saved* Israel from the death with which Pharoah would have visited her.

Thus, in concrete historical circumstances many times experienced in the history of God's people, were born the ideas of deliverance, ransom, redemption and salvation. Nowadays these ideas appear unintelligible to many of our contemporaries, because they do not relate them to the circumstances in which they were brought into being. To the ears of those who have forgotten the historical origins of the words, they are just a 'religious noise', relics of a 'prelogical' mentality. But now more than one people has experienced an occupation and a liberation, which may help again to give people understanding of the meaning of biblical ideas.

St. Paul was familiar enough with the ransoming of slaves, *apolutrosis*, and he carried the term over into theology to express the setting-free of man that Christ brought about. It is this concrete term which has given the words *redemptio* in Latin and 'redemption' in English.

Israel was to experience servitude, captivity, oppression and deliverance not once but many times. And each time she was set free by a man whom God raised up for that purpose, a man 'after his own heart'. So the idea of a deliverer, a saviour, also was born as a result of actual experiences.

After Israel had taken possession of the Promised Land, she 'waxed fat', and forsook the God who had watched over her and brought her out of the land of Egypt. Her people deserted the covenant with God and turned to vain idols, worshipping that which did not exist. Then God raised up a people to chastise the faithless Israelites and to mistreat them as Pharoah had done.

And now the sons of Israel defied the Lord to his face, and began to worship the gods of the country-side. Not for them the Lord God of their fathers, who had rescued them from Egypt; they must have new gods to worship, gods of the nations that dwelt around them; they must challenge the Lord's anger by paying court to Baal and Astaroth instead.

Thus angered, the Lord left Israel at the mercy of invaders who plundered them, betrayed them to those enemies of theirs who lived round about. No longer could they make head against their adversaries; march where they would, the Lord still fought against them, true to his threat, true to the oath he had taken, and it fared ill indeed with them.

Sometimes he would send them chieftains of their own, to rescue them from the invader's power, but even to these they would not listen; still they would play the wanton, and worship alien gods; so quick were they to forsake their fathers' ways, and disobey the Lord's known will. First a chieftain would arise, and the Lord, in his days, would relent; would listen to the plaint of a people in distress, and save them from the threat of destruction; then, once he was dead, the sons would prove worse than their fathers before them; would pay court to alien gods, and enslave themselves to alien worship; still they would not leave their false imaginings, the rebellious path they trod (Judges 2: 11–19)

The pattern was repeated throughout Israel's history as God imposed trial after trial on his people.

The men of Israel . . . defied the Lord's will, forsook him, their own God, and paid court instead to the gods of the countryside, and to Astaroth; and the Lord, in high displeasure against Israel, left them at the mercy of Chusan-Rasathaim, king of the Mesopotamian land, who for eight years became their master.

Then they cried out to the Lord, and he sent a champion to their rescue . . . (Judges 3: 7–9; cf. chs. 4, 6, 10, 13)

The men whom Yahweh raised up to deliver Israel spoke in Yahweh's name. That is what is meant by the word *nabhi*, 'prophet': not so much one who foretells what is to come, as one who speaks the word of God; he explains the *meaning* of what is happening, interprets the significance of history, and shows God's will to his people. 'Early to your doors the Lord sent all those prophets that were servants of his, but hearing there was none, nor heeding' (Jer. 25: 4). The *nabhi* is a man on whom God's spirit rests, an 'inspired' man (Hosea 9: 7): 'Make choice of Josue the son of Nun . . . lay thy hand upon him' (Num.

27: 18); 'Then they cried out to the Lord, and he sent a champion to their rescue, Othoniel . . . On him the Lord's spirit fell, and he became the ruler of Israel' (Judges 3: 9, 10); 'The Spirit of the Lord wrapped Gedeon round'; 'The Spirit of the Lord was with Jephte wherever he went'; 'The Spirit of the Lord first visited him [Samson]'; 'The Spirit of the Lord came down upon Samson' (Judges 6: 34, 11: 29, 13: 25, 14: 6).

The book of Deuteronomy (18: 15–18) puts this famous prediction into the mouth of Moses: 'The Lord thy God will raise up for thee a prophet like myself, of thy own race, a brother of thy own; it is to him thou must listen. Was it not thy own plea, that day when all were publicly assembled at mount Horeb, that thou mightest hear the voice of the Lord thy God no longer, have sight of that raging fire no longer, lest it should be thy death? And the Lord told me, All that they have said is well said. I will raise up for them a prophet like thyself, one of their own race, entrusting my own message to his lips, so that he may instruct them at my bidding.' The prophet among us is a blessing, not only because God speaks through him, but also because he spares us from hearing the voice of God ourselves, for that would be too much for us. No man can see God and live. It is his goodness that withholds sight of himself from us, lest we should die.

The time came when Israel wanted to have a king. 'as other nations have'. 'So all the elders of Israel met Samuel at Ramatha; . . . they said to him ". . . Give us a king, such as other nations have, to sit in judgement over us." It was little to Samuel's mind . . . but when he betook himself to the Lord in prayer, the Lord said to him, "Grant the people all they ask of thee. It is my rule over them they are casting off, not thine. It has ever been the same, since the day when I rescued them from Egypt; me they will ever be forsaking, to worship other gods; and now it is thy turn"' (1 Kings 8: 4–8).

This same demand has already appeared in the book of Judges (8: 22–23): 'Now all the Israelites would have Gedeon, the man who delivered them from Madian, become their ruler, and his descendants after him. Neither I, he said, nor any son of mine shall bear rule over you; the Lord shall be your ruler.' Samuel in his turn set the position and rights of a king before the people: 'He will take away your sons from you, to drive his chariots; he will need horsemen . . . ploughmen and reapers, armourers and wheelwrights. It is your daughters that will make his perfumes, and cook for him, and bake for him. All the best of your lands and vineyards and olive-yards he will take away . . . and he will tithe the revenues of such crop and vintage as is left you . . . He will take away servants and handmaids of yours, . . . of your herds, too, he will take tithe. You will be his slaves.' But they would not listen to Samuel: 'That will not serve, they cried out, a king, we must have a king!' (1 Kings 8: 11–20).

Samuel called the children of Israel together at Mizpah, 'and this message he gave them from the Lord God of Israel: "It was I that rescued you from Egypt, I that protected you from the clutches of these and of all your oppressors. And now you have cast away your God, your only shield against so many misfortunes and afflictions; A king, you say, appoint a king to reign over us!" (1 Kings 10: 18–19); 'Nothing would serve but that I should appoint a king to command you; as if the Lord your God were not reigning among you as your king!' (1 Kings 12: 12); 'When I call upon the Lord's name, he will . . . give you visible proof of the great wrong you have done by defying him and asking for a king' (1 Kings 12: 17). 'The whole people cried out with one voice, "Pray to the Lord thy God for us thy servants, that our lives may be spared? We have sinned enough already, and now we have done him further wrong, by asking for a king to rule us"' (1 Kings 12: 19).

Nevertheless, the Lord did as the Israelites wanted and gave them a king. 'The day before Saul's coming, the Lord warned Samuel privately, "At this time of day to-morrow I am sending a man of Benjamin on an errand to thee. He it is thou must anoint to be king of my people Israel; he is to deliver them from the power of the Philistines. Their plaints have not gone unheard, nor unheeded".' *Etiam peccata.* God salvages and makes use even of his people's sins to forward his work. 'And now Samuel took out his phial of oil, and poured it out over Saul's head; then he kissed him, and said, "Hereby the Lord anoints thee to be the leader of his chosen people . . . The spirit of the Lord will fall upon thee, making thee prophesy with the rest, and turning thee into a new man. . . .'' So parted Saul from Samuel, and as he went on his way, the Lord gave him a new heart . . . the spirit of the Lord fell on him, and he prophesied with the rest' (1 Kings 9: 15–16, 10: 1–10).

In the Bible, oil is the sign and sacrament of the Spirit. The priestly consecration of Aaron was done by anointing with oil: 'And then anoint his head with oil; so shall he be consecrated' (Exodus 29: 7; cf. Lev. 8: 30). It is 'the oil of your consecration' (Lev. 10: 7); the high priest is 'anointed' (Num. 35: 25). David's kingly consecration was done in the same way. Yahweh said to Samuel, 'Up, anoint him; for this is my choice.' And Samuel took the horn of oil 'and anointed him then and there in his brethren's presence; and on him, on David, the spirit of the Lord

The anointing of David
(Byzantine psalter of sixteenth century)

came down, ever after that day' (1 Kings 16: 12–13); 'Here was my servant David; on him my consecrating oil has been poured' (Ps. 88: 21 [89: 20]). The same with Solomon: ' With a phial of oil brought out from the tabernacle, the priest Sadoc anointed Solomon king ' (3 [1] Kings 1: 39).

One anointed of the Lord was called in Hebrew *mashiah* (commonly anglicized as 'messiah'), from the verb *mashah*, to anoint. This is the word that was translated into Greek as *khristos*, from the verb *khrio*, having the same meaning.

It is necessary thus briefly to recall the factors that explain the concrete historical origin of the idea of a messiah, a deliverer, a saviour, in order to understand Israel's messianic hope, which was fulfilled in Jesus Christ. Election or choice by God, sin, captivity, release by God's hand raising up a man after his own heart, a man anointed of the Spirit to effect this deliverance: the experience of these things by the Israelites gradually built up the idea of *the* deliverance, a definitive and total setting-free, by a Saviour of whom Moses, the Judges and David were only 'types' —prophetical figures.

It must be noticed that Israel's messianic hope represents the the hope of all mankind, which became conscious of itself in and through Israel. This hope of the Jewish people is not a passing curiosity, of interest only in the history of religions: it concerns the whole of mankind, it invites philosophical analysis, because it is, implicitly, universal. The *desiderium naturale* that haunts all human kind finds its fullest and most developed form in the looking forward to the Messiah among those specially perceptive people, the Jews. It is not Israel alone who looks for the Saviour, but all mankind, the whole travailing creation. Their prayer is given voice by Israel, the head of the nations (Jer. 31: 7), moved thereto by the Spirit. It is this cosmic hope that the prophets expressed, and after them St. Paul; its full extent and scope could be made clear only in the coming of Him who brings fullness, towards whom the desire of all creation reaches out.

From the stock of Jesse a scion shall burgeon yet; out of his roots a flower shall spring. One shall be born, on whom the spirit of the Lord will rest; a spirit wise and discerning, a spirit prudent and strong, a spirit of knowledge and of piety, and ever fear of the Lord shall fill his heart . . . here is judgement will give the poor redress, here is award will right the wrongs of the defenceless. . . .

Love of right shall be the baldric he wears, faithfulness the strength that girds him. Wolf shall live at peace with lamb, leopard take its ease with kid. . . . All over this mountain, my sanctuary, no hurt shall be done, no life taken. Deep as the waters that hide the sea-floor, knowledge of the Lord overspreading the world!

There he stands, fresh root from Jesse's stem, signal beckoning to the peoples all around; the Gentiles will come to pay their homage, where he rests in glory. Then, once again, the Lord's hand at work! From Assyria, from Egypt . . . from the islands out at sea, his people, a scattered remnant, shall return.

High lifted, for a world to see it, the standard that shall call Israel home, gather in the exiled sons of Juda from the four corners of the earth. (Isa. 11: 1–12)

'A root out of Jesse'
(Biblia Pauperum, 15th century)

'A star out of Jacob'

THE INCARNATION

' . . . the appointed time came. Then God sent out his Son on a mission to us. He took birth from a woman . . . so as to . . . make us sons by adoption' (Gal. 4: 4–5).

If God was to come amongst us it was needful that mankind

be ready to receive him; his incarnation could not happen at just any moment of time: he had to prepare a people among whom he could appear. That people was Israel. But neither could the Incarnation happen at just any moment in Israel's history; she had to be spiritually ready to welcome her Lord. And his incarnation could not take place without the consent and agreement of mankind being expressed in the person of one of its members at least. It was in a woman, the Virgin Mary, that the human race was pre-adapted to receive God, that is to say, made holy to receive the Holy One. Mary's divine motherhood implied and required in advance the essential holiness of the maiden of Israel who should say mankind's 'Yes' to the Lord, and consent to receive him within herself.

And it was necessary that certain general human conditions should be fulfilled before the Incarnation could come about. If it had happened amidst some tribe or other during paleolithic times, the world would never have heard anything about it. The Good News would not have been able to be spread abroad, not only because there was no soil suitable to receive it, but also because man had not yet reached an age and a state of unification which would allow God's word to be the leaven of the human mixture. Mankind had to be physically ready to receive the seed; before that, the preaching of the Gospel would have been premature. That is why the Bible attaches so much importance to 'time'.

In order, then that the Incarnation might truly transform man and the Gospel be carried to the ends of the earth, there had to be in existence a certain determined level of ethnic, psychological, social and economic conditions. The Incarnation in fact took place at the moment when the Roman empire had made a unity of the Mediterranean world. 'It has been said, well before Bossuet, that the unity of the empire was a wonderful help to the spread of the Gospel. But even this Roman unity, which was to become Christian unity, was itself an inheritance, at any rate as regards the eastern end of the Mediterranean. Hellenism had prepared things here, in the person of Alexander' (A. J. Festugière, *Le monde gréco-romain au temps de Notre-Seigneur*,

Vol. I, Paris, 1935). A common language, Greek, was also a basic factor.

Another important aspect of material development that helped the diffusion of the Gospel was the centralized road-system. 'One central government and the fixed principles of imperial policy kept this vast empire and its very diverse parts together. But this administrative unity would not have been possible had the countries concerned not been able to communicate with one another, and with Rome, by means of a complete system of land and sea routes. It was these routes that the Apostles followed. Thanks to the work of the legionaries, they could move with ease across the highlands of Asia Minor, where today there are only a few rough tracks' (*ibid.*, pp. 14–15). 'The importance of the material resources available to the Apostles can hardly be exaggerated. The more one looks into it, the more one realizes how right St. Paul was when he said that the Gospel was being preached at just the right moment, when the physical world itself had been got ready for it' (*ibid.*, p. 20).

Jesus Christ came among men knowing that he would suffer and die by man's hand. The prophets of Israel, acting and speaking in the Lord's name, had experienced man's resistance to God's call, to his invitation, to his will; from Moses onwards, every *nabhi* had denounced the Chosen People's recalcitrance to the transfiguring and saving work of the Spirit: 'Stiff-necked race, your heart and ears still uncircumcised, you are for ever resisting the Holy Spirit, just as your fathers did. There was not one of the prophets they did not persecute' (Acts 7: 51–52). The Israelite's opposition to God's work in their midst is the opposition of all mankind: the world manifests it today, as the Jews manifested it then. It is our refusal of God's will that makes a transformation, a supernaturalization, so necessary, a new birth that is bound to be painful in its first phase.

And so the prophets were persecuted: 'Jerusalem, Jerusalem, still murdering the prophets, and stoning the messengers that are sent to thee, how often have I been ready to gather thy children together, as a hen gathers her chickens under her wings, and thou didst refuse it!' (Matt. 23: 37; Luke 13: 34). 'They

shall fight against thee . . .'
God told Jeremiah (1 : 19), and
in this conflict the prophets'
weapon was the two-edged
sword of God's word.

Christ's inevitable sufferings
were foretold in the very life of
the prophets, before even they
uttered them by their tongues;
their lives were as prophetical
as their words. 'God has fulfilled in this way what was foretold by all the prophets about
the sufferings of his Christ'
(Acts 3: 18; cf. 17: 3, 26: 23;
Luke 24: 46).

Moses, the Judges, David
were prophetical types of him
who was to come, but the fulfilment of the messianic hope
was not merely a repetition of
what had been shown forth by
these men in Israel's history.
The coming of Christ intro-
duced an essentially new
dimension. The hope was fulfilled in this unlooked for gift
of God which was beyond all
understanding—man's heart
has not conceived the things
which God has prepared for
those who love him. Mankind
longs for God, the everlasting
super-natural newness of life.

Had Christ been no more
than Israel's temporal deliverer, analogous to Moses or the

*Isaiah and St. Matthew:
the Old Testament carrying the New
(Chartres)*

Judges or David, he would have repeated, done again, that which they had done prophetically: but he would not have *fulfilled* the hope. Such a repetition of what had gone before would have been in itself a sign of the event's falling short of the hope. It was the very *newness*, essentially supernatural, of the Incarnation that was a stumbling-block to those who were looking for a repetition of what had already been. When it came, the gift went infinitely beyond all hope and expectation, because it was God himself who was given.

The weakness of Jesus in the eyes of the world and the opposition he encountered are in direct line with the thought of Israel's prophets, for whom the immediate and unqualified triumph of a martial messiah would have been a sure sign of his falsity. This dialectic of failure and success, of success in and through failure, is a constant element in Israel's history and in all biblical thought. It is to be found in Israel's very constitution: 'If the Lord has held you closely to him and shewed you special favour, it was not that you overshadowed other peoples in greatness; of all nations you are the smallest' (Deut. 7: 7). Could not great nations, in all the glory of their power, their civilization, their achievements and their wealth, ask of little Israel, as she was to ask about Jesus, 'Who is this, that we should bow down?'

In Judah was God made known. What Isaiah said of Yahweh's servant must be said of Israel: 'He will watch this servant of his appear among us, unregarded as brushwood shoot, as a plant in waterless soil; no stateliness here, no majesty, no beauty, as we gaze upon him, to win our hearts. Nay, here is one despised, left out of all human reckoning, bowed with misery, and no stranger to weakness; . . . How should we take any account of him, a man so despised?' (Isa. 53: 2–3).

Like the greatness of Jesus, Israel's greatness is of another order. She does not strike the world's eye, she is an enigma to worldly wisdom. It is the dialectic we keep on meeting in sacred history. 'In you shall all the nations of the earth be blessed': that promise was made to a man, to Abraham, an emigrant, a 'stateless person'. In the struggles between peoples,

Israel always exemplified this dialectic of weakness overcoming strength through Yahweh's aid. The nations trusted in their riches and might, Egypt relied on her chariots and horsemen, but Israel put her trust in the name of the Lord. To Gedeon, going out to war against the troops of Madian, Yahweh gave the pattern that was to endure: '"This is a great army thou hast with thee," the Lord told Gedeon. "I must not grant victory over Madian to an army like this, or the Israelites would boast that they had no need of me; that their own strength had brought them deliverance"' (Judges 7:2). God always baffles our wisdom, those calculations of ours that we base on what the world calls power and not on his power. The whole of Israel's history is a demonstration of God's strength finding 'its full scope in weakness', as he said to Paul (2 Cor. 12:9); her continued existence is a standing verification of it, the prophets continually repeat it, and young David says to Goliath of Gath, 'Though thou comest with sword and spear and shield to meet me, meet the I will, in the name of the Lord . . .' (1 Kings 17:45).

Had Jesus come in the strength and power of this world, he certainly would not have come as having anything to do with the God of Israel. The victory of Jesus was his resurrection, and he came to it only through the failure of the cross. 'A grain of wheat must fall into the ground and die, or else it remains nothing more than a grain of wheat . . .' (John 12:24).

> Yours is to be the same mind which Christ Jesus shewed. His nature is, from the first, divine, and yet he did not see, in the rank of Godhead, a prize to be coveted; he dispossessed himself, and took the nature of a slave, fashioned in the likeness of men, and presenting himself to us in human form; and then he lowered his own dignity, accepted an obedience which brought him to death, death on a cross.
>
> That is why God has raised him to such a height, given him that name which is greater than any other name;
>
> so that everything in heaven and on earth and under the earth must bend the knee before the name of Jesus,
>
> and every tongue must confess JESUS CHRIST AS THE LORD, dwelling in the glory of God the Father. (Phil. 2: 5–11)

PAUL
WORKER WITH GOD

The Lord Jesus Christ said of himself, 'My errand is only to the lost sheep that are of the house of Israel'; and to the Twelve, when he sent them out for the first time, 'Do not go,' he said, 'into the walks of the Gentiles, or enter any city of Samaria; go rather to the lost sheep that belong to the house of Israel' (Matt. 15: 24, 10: 5–6). There is an order, a 'plan', in the economy of God's salvation. Knowledge of him and of his saving work begins with Israel—salvation comes from the Jews; and it is from them that knowledge of God has to spread to the peoples of the whole earth.

So he is proclaimed a first time, to Israel; and a second time, to all the world. After his resurrection, the Lord commands the Apostles: 'You, therefore, must go out, making disciples of all nations, and baptizing them in the name of the Father, and of the Son, and of the Holy Ghost, teaching them to observe all the commandments which I have given you. And behold I am with you all through the days that are coming, until the consummation of the world' (Matt. 28: 19); 'Go out all over the world, and preach the gospel to the whole of creation' (Mark 16: 15).

The book of Acts (8: 1–17) relates how the persecution that followed Stephen's stoning led to a scattering of Hellenist Christians, with happy consequences: 'The Church in Jerusalem was much persecuted at this time, and all except the apostles were scattered about over the country-side of Judaea and Samaria. . . . Those who had been driven away spread the gospel as they went from place to place; and Philip, who had gone down to one of the cities of Samaria, preached Christ there. The multitude listened with general accord to what Philip said, as their own eyes and ears witnessed the miracles he did. . . . And now the apostles at Jerusalem, hearing that Samaria had received the word of God, sent Peter and John to visit them. So these two came down and prayed for them, that they might receive the Holy Spirit, who had not, as yet, come down on any of them; they had received nothing so far except baptism in the name of the Lord Jesus. Then the apostles began to lay their hands on them, so that the Holy Spirit was given them.'

'No doubt,' writes M. Goguel,* 'this was the first mission in the Judaean region around Jerusalem. Its beginnings were very early, being anterior to Paul's conversion. Information about this Hellenist mission is very fragmentary. For instance, we know nothing about the circumstances in which the Church was founded at Damascus. We learn of its existence there from the account of Paul's conversion (Acts 9), and it is natural to suppose

---

* *La naissance du Christianisme* (Paris, 1944), p. 202.

it was a result of the Hellenist mission. Nor do we know anything about the activities of those who went to Phoenicia and Cyprus, or how the church of Caesarea was founded; we may, however, conjecture from Acts 8: 40 and 21: 8 that this last was Philip's work '.

The conversion of the centurion Cornelius marks an important stage in the growth of the young Church, when she stretched out her arms to the heathen.

> Thereupon Peter began speaking; 'I see clearly enough,' he said, 'that God makes no distinction between man and man; he welcomes anybody, whatever his race, who fears him and does

what piety demands. God has sent his word to the sons of
Israel, giving them news of peace through Jesus Christ, who is
Lord of all. You have heard the story, a story which ran through
the whole of Judaea, though it began in Gallilee, after the baptism which John proclaimed; about Jesus of Nazareth, how God
anointed him with the Holy Spirit and with power, so that he
went about doing good, and curing all those who were under
the devil's tyranny, with God at his side. We are witnesses of
all he did in the country of the Jews, and in Jerusalem. And
they killed him, hanging him on a gibbet; but on the third day
God raised him up again, and granted the clear sight of him, not
to the people at large, but to us, the witnesses whom God had
appointed beforehand; we ate and drank in his company after
his rising from the dead. And he gave us a commission to
preach to the people, and to bear witness that he, and none other,
has been chosen by God to judge the living and the dead. All
the prophets bear him this testimony, that everyone who has
faith in him is to find remission of sins through his name.'

Before Peter had finished speaking to them thus, the Holy
Spirit fell on all those who were listening to his message. The
faithful who had come over with Peter, holding to the tradition
of circumcision as they did, were astonished to find that the
free gift of the Holy Spirit could be lavished upon the Gentiles,
whom they heard speaking with tongues, and proclaiming the
greatness of God. Then Peter said openly, 'Who will grudge
us the water for baptizing these men, that have received the
Holy Spirit just as we did?' And he gave orders that they should
be baptized in the name of the Lord. . . .

And now the apostles and brethren in Judaea were told how
the word of God had been given to the Gentiles. And when
Peter came up to Jerusalem, those who held to the tradition of
circumcision found fault with him; 'Why didst thou pay a visit,'
they asked, 'to men who are uncircumcised, and eat with them?'
Whereupon Peter told them the story point by point from the
beginning . . . (Acts 10: 34–49, 11: 1 ff.)

Peter ends his account of the conversion of Cornelius with
these words: 'And then, when I had set about speaking to them,
the Holy Spirit fell upon them, just as it was with us at the beginning. Then I was reminded of what the Lord said to us;
John's baptism was with water, but there is a baptism with the

Holy Spirit which you are to receive. And now, if God has made them the same free gift, which he made to us when faith in the Lord Jesus had gone before it, who was I, what power had I, to stay God's hand?'

The Jerusalem community was convinced: 'At these words, they were content, and gave glory to God; "Why then," they said, "it seems God has granted life-giving repentance of heart to the Gentiles too".' (Acts 11: 15–18).

FOUNDATION OF THE CHURCH AT ANTIOCH

In the same book of Acts (11 : 19–21) it is written: 'Meanwhile, those who had been dispersed owing to the persecution that was raised over Stephen had travelled as far away as Phoenice and Cyprus and Antioch, without preaching the word to anyone except the Jews. But there were some of them, men of Cyprus and Cyrene, who, when they found their way to Antioch, spoke to the Greeks as well, preaching the Lord Jesus to them. And the Lord's power went with them, so that a great number learned to believe, and turned to the Lord.'

To quote M. Goguel again (*op. cit.*, p. 207): 'The importance of the establishment of Christianity in Antioch must be emphasized, for this was the third city of the empire and the principal one in the prefecture of The East. Christianity now for the first time got a footing in one of the metropolitan centres of the ancient world; the Church was established in a place which, through its world-wide communications and connexions, was to become one of the chief points of radiation for the new religion.'

As had been done in the case of the mission in Samaria, the Church in Jerusalem at once sent one of the brethren to Antioch.

The story of this came to the ears of the Church at Jerusalem, and they sent Barnabas on a mission to Antioch. When he came there and saw what grace God was bestowing on them, he was full of joy, and encouraged them all to remain true to the Lord with steady purpose of heart, like the good man he was, full of the Holy Spirit, full of faith; a great multitude was thus won over to the Lord. He went on to Tarsus, to look for Saul, and when he found him, brought him back to Antioch. For a whole year after this they were made welcome in the Church there, teaching a great multitude. And Antioch was the first place in which the disciples were called Christians. (Acts 11 : 22–26)

We are told furthermore that, at the time of the famine under Claudius in the year 44, it was Barnabas and Saul who were commissioned to take relief from the brethren at Antioch to those in Judaea. 'Barnabas and Saul returned from Jerusalem, their mission fulfilled, and took John, also called Mark, in their company' (Acts 11 : 29–30; 12 : 25).

Antioch on the Orontes

Seleucia

FIRST MISSIONARY JOURNEY

(about 45–49)

The Church at Antioch had as its prophets and teachers Barnabas, and Simon who was called Niger, and Lucius of Cyrene, and Manahen, foster-brother of Herod the tetrarch, and Saul. These were offering worship to God and fasting, when the Holy Spirit said, 'I must have Barnabas and Saul dedicated to the work to which I have called them.' Thereupon they fasted and prayed and laid their hands on them, and so took leave of them.

And they, sent on their travels by the Holy Spirit, went down to Seleucia, and from there took ship for Cyprus. So they reached Salamis, where they preached God's word in the Jewish synagogues; they had John, too, to help them. And when they had been through the whole island up to Paphos, they encountered there a magician who claimed to be a prophet, a Jew named Bar-Jesus. He was in the company of the governor, Sergius Paulus, a man of good sense, who had sent for Barnabas and Saul and asked if he might hear the word of God. And Elymas, the magician (that is what his name means when translated), opposed them, trying to turn the governor away from the faith. (Acts 13: 1–8)

After this Paul and his companions took ship from Paphos and made for Perge in Pamphylia; here John left them, and went back to Jerusalem. They passed on from Perge, and reached Pisidian Antioch, where they went and took their seats in the synagogue on the sabbath day . . . (Acts 13: 13–14)

'They took ship for Cyprus' (Acts 13: 4).
(Capitoline Museum, Rome)

Paphos:
church and pillar called Saint Paul's

But the Jews used influence with such women of fashion as worshipped the true God, and with the leading men in the city, setting on foot a persecution against Paul and Barnabas and driving them out of their territory; so they shook off the dust from their feet as they left them, and went on to Iconium. The disciples, meanwhile, were filled with rejoicing, and with the Holy Spirit. (Acts 13: 50–52)

While they were at Iconium, they went into the Jewish synagogue together, and preached in such a way that a great number both of Jews and of Greeks found faith, although the Jews who would not believe stirred up trouble among the Gentiles and poisoned their minds against the brethren. For a long time, then, they remained there, speaking boldly in the Lord's name, while he attested the preaching of his grace by allowing signs and wonders to be performed by their means; the common folk of the city were divided in opinion, some taking part with the Jews, and some with the apostles. Then, when both Gentiles and Jews, in concert with their rulers, made a movement to assault and stone them, they thought it best to take refuge in the Lycaonian cities, Lystra and Derbe, and the country round them; and they preached the gospel there. (Acts 14: 1–7)

Iconium

At Lystra, Paul cured a man who was not able to use his feet.

The multitudes, seeing what Paul had done, cried out in the Lycaonian dialect, 'It is the gods, who have come down to us in human shape.' They called Barnabas Jupiter, and Paul Mercury, because he was the chief speaker; and the priest of Jupiter, Defender of the City, brought out bulls and wreaths to the gates, eager, like the multitude, to do sacrifice.

The apostles tore their garments when they heard of it; and both Barnabas and Paul ran out among the multitude, crying aloud: 'Sirs, why are you doing all this? We too are mortal men like yourselves; the whole burden of our preaching is that you

The road to Lystra

must turn away from follies like this to the worship of the living God, who made sky and earth and sea and all that is in them. . . .' (Acts 14: 10–14)

But some of the Jews from Antioch and Iconium had followed them; these won over the multitude to their side, and they stoned Paul and dragged him out of the city, leaving him there for dead. But the disciples formed a ring about him, and soon he rose up and went back into the city; next day he left, with Barnabas, for Derbe. In that city too they preached, and made many disciples; then they returned to Lystra, Iconium and Antioch, where they fortified the spirits of the disciples, encouraging them to be true to the faith, and telling them that we cannot enter the kingdom of heaven without many trials. Then, with fasting and prayer, they appointed presbyters for them in each of the churches, and commended them to the care of the Lord in whom they had learned to believe. So they passed through Pisidia, and reached Pamphylia. They preached the word of the Lord in Perge, and went down to Attalia, taking ship there for Antioch, where they had been committed to God's grace for the work they had now achieved. On their arrival, they called the Church together, and told the story of all God had done to aid them, and how, through faith, he had left a door open for the Gentiles. And they stayed there a considerable time with the disciples. (Acts 14: 18–27)

PREACHING IN THE SYNAGOGUE

As we have seen, whenever he came to a town, Paul first went to the Jewish synagogue, there to proclaim God's word; he used the method that had been followed from the Church's very birth. Salvation comes from the Jews, and it was only right that they should be the people first to hear the Good News of the coming of him who makes all things new.

They passed on from Perge, and reached Pisidian Antioch, where they went and took their seats in the synagogue on the sabbath day. When the reading from the law and the prophets was finished, the rulers of the synagogue sent a message to them to say, 'Brethren, if you have in your hearts any word of encouragement for the people, let us hear it.'

Paul preaching in a synagogue
(13th century)

Then Paul stood up, and made a gesture with his hand to claim audience. 'Listen,' he said, 'men of Israel, and all you who worship the true God. The God of this people of Israel chose out our fathers, and made his people great at the time when they were strangers in the land of Egypt, stretching out his arm to deliver them from it. For forty years he bore with their hard hearts in the wilderness; then he overthrew seven nations in the land of Chanaan, whose lands he gave them for an inheritance. By now, some four hundred and fifty years had passed; and after this he appointed judges over them, up to the time of the prophet Samuel. Then they asked for a king, and God gave them Saul, son of Cis, a man of the tribe of Benjamin, who reigned forty years; but afterwards dispossessed him, and raised up David to be their king. To him, he gave this testimony, "I have found in David, son of Jesse, a man after my own heart, who will accomplish all that is my will."

'It is out of this man's posterity, according to the promise made to him, that God has brought us a Saviour, Jesus. John had prepared the way for his coming, by proclaiming a baptism in which all the people of Israel was to repent; but John himself, when he was coming to the end of his life's course, told them, "I am not what you suspect me to be; look rather for one who comes after me; I am not worthy to untie the shoes on his feet."

'Brethren, you who are sons of Abraham, and you others who fear God, this message of salvation is sent to you. The people at Jerusalem, like their rulers, did not recognize Jesus for what he was; unwittingly they fulfilled, by condemning him, those utterances of the prophets which they had heard read, sabbath after sabbath. And although they could find no capital charge against him, they petitioned Pilate for his death. So, when they had fulfilled all that had been written about him, they took him down from the cross and laid him in a tomb. And, on the third day, God raised him from the dead. He was seen, over a space of many days, by the men who had come up with him from Galilee to Jerusalem; it is they who now bear witness of him before the people.

'And this is the message we preach to you; there was a promise made to our forefathers, and this promise God has redeemed for our posterity, by raising Jesus to life. Thus, it is written in the second Psalm, "Thou art my Son; I have begotten thee this day." And this is how he describes raising him from the dead, never to return to corruption again, "I will grant you the privileges I have promised to David"; to which purpose he says in another psalm, "Thou wilt not allow thy faithful servant to see corruption".' (Acts 13: 14–35)

On the following sabbath almost all the city had assembled to hear God's word. The Jews, when they saw these crowds, were full of indignation, and began to argue blasphemously against all that Paul said. Whereupon Paul and Barnabas told them roundly, 'We were bound to preach God's words to you first; but now, since you reject it, since you declare yourselves unfit for eternal life, be it so; we will turn our thoughts to the Gentiles. This, after all, is the charge the Lord has given us, "I have appointed thee to be a light for the Gentiles, that thou mayst bring salvation to the ends of the earth".' (Acts 13: 44–47)

At Iconium, 'they went into the Jewish synagogue together, and preached in such a way that a great number both of Jews and of Greeks found faith'; 'They . . . reached Thessalonica. Here the Jews had a synagogue, and Paul, as his custom was, paid them a visit there. Over a space of three sabbaths he reasoned with them out of the scriptures, expounding these and bringing proofs from them that the sufferings of Christ and his rising from the dead were fore-ordained; "the Christ", he said, "is none other than the Jesus whom I am preaching to you".' At Beroea, 'as soon as they arrived, they made their way to the Jewish synagogue. These were of a better breed than the Thessalonians; they welcomed the word with all eagerness, and examined the Scriptures, day after day, to find out whether all this was true.' (Acts 14: 1; 17: 1–3, 10 ff.)

At Corinth, 'every sabbath he held a disputation in the synagogue, trying to convince both Jews and Greeks . . . Just at the time when Silas and Timothy arrived from Macedonia, Paul was much occupied with preaching, while he bore witness to the Jews that Jesus was the Christ. But they set their faces against it and talked blasphemy, until he shook the dust out of his garments, and said to them, "Your blood be upon your own heads, I am clear of it; I will go the Gentiles henceforeward".' At Ephesus, 'he himself went to the synagogue and reasoned with the Jews.' Finally, at Rome he gathered the leaders of the Jews together, and many of them came to the house where he lodged. To them, Paul 'bore his testimony and told them about the kingdom of God, trying to convince them from Moses and the prophets of what Jesus was, from dawn till dusk. Some were convinced by his words, others refused belief; and they took their leave, still at variance among themselves.' But not before Paul had told them, 'Take notice, then, that this message of salvation has been sent by God to the Gentiles, and they, at least, will listen to it' (Acts 18: 4–6, 19; 28: 23 ff.).

ISRAEL AND THE NATIONS

God's economy of salvation was first to constitute a holy people as the first-fruits of the sanctification of all mankind, a leaven to work in the whole human race, a people fit to be carriers

D

λαιιου σαγιωῆ· ἱερυτορι
ἐσάγχρουσαϊωτρία. Ε
αcοῦ βυμεόθιόρον ✝
K φιδιότορ ἁγο ιεατα ικαὶ
ιιαο ιεαϊ πο λϲc. διδαϊ
ο ιεαορ ιεαϊ πορεϊαγ ποι
οῦ μβροc ϟοι λῆιι ✝

of knowledge of himself. 'It is in Juda God makes himself known' (Ps. 75 [76]: 1); 'Of what use is it, then, to be a Jew? What value was there in circumcision? Much, I answer, in every respect; chiefly because the Jews had the words of God entrusted to them' (Rom. 3: 1–2). The making supernatural of the whole of mankind was to spread from this one particular existing people.

At no moment in human history, and by means of no people whatever, could the knowledge of God be imposed from outside on a mankind not ready to receive it. Knowledge of God, which is salvation, had to be born in mankind, that is, to appear at a determined time and in a particular place, and then gradually to spread to the whole human race. There had to be a soil that was ready for this knowledge, a part of mankind prepared for the coming of this revelation, a particular people to whom God made himself known, transforming and hallowing it so that it should be a fit receptacle for the revelation. This part of mankind was Israel. Like all creation and all birth, the people of God began with a germinal bud, a shoot, and for mankind at large this bud of salvation was the Jewish people. 'What is there that bears a likeness to the kingdom of heaven; what comparison shall I find for it? It is like a grain of mustard seed, that a man has taken and planted in his garden, where it has thriven and grown into a great tree, and all the birds have come and settled in its branches.' (Luke 13: 18–19). "Of all seeds, none is so little, but when it grows up it is greater than any garden herb; it grows into a tree . . .' (Matt. 13: 32).

The prophets call the Messiah The Shoot, who shall spring up and rebuild the Lord's Temple.* The people of God, Christ's living dwelling-place, share in this seminal nature of Christ, in whom all has been created, and will continue to be created until the consummation of time.

THE LAW

When God constituted a particular people in whom he would make himself known, and through whom mankind at large should be transformed, he set up a dialectic between this germinal people and the rest of peoples.

A law was the necessary mould for Israel; amid the corruptions of heathendom, a holy people was not possible without a binding charter to regenerate mind and will. The Mosaic Law was regenerative, and two parts can be discerned in it.

One part represents that continuing requirement of holiness that binds all men in all times: not to prostitute himself to idols made by his own hands or spun out of his own thoughts, not to sacrifice his children to Baals and Molochs and 'reasons of state', not to kill, not to deceive—such requirements are elementary and without their observance no holiness at all is possible. These ordinances of the Law of Moses are written in the conscience of every human being.

> There will be affliction then and distress for every human soul that has practised wickedness, the Jew in the first instance, but the Gentile too; there will be glory and honour and peace for everyone who has done good, the Jew in the first instance, but the Gentile too. There are no human preferences with God. Those who have been sinners without regard to the law will be doomed without regard to the law; those who have been sinners with the law for their rule will be judged with the law for their rule. To have heard the law read out is no claim to acceptance

---

* See Zach. 3: 8; 6: 12. The Hebrew has Shoot or Branch, but the Greek is ambiguous, hence the differing translations in various English versions: Branch, Dayspring, Orient, Rising Sun, etc. Cf. Isa. 4: 2; Jer. 23: 5.

with God; it is those who obey the law who will be justified. As for the Gentiles, though they have no law to guide them, there are times when they carry out the precepts of the law unbidden, finding in their own natures a rule to guide them, in default of any other rule; and this shews that the obligations of the law are written in their hearts; their conscience utters its own testimony, and when they dispute with one another they find themselves condemning this, approving that. (Rom. 2: 9–15)

The other part of the Law of Moses has not this universal and timeless character. It consists of precepts, rites and observances which had a very important purpose and function for Israel at a certain epoch and in view of certain circumstances, notably the relation of God's people to the surrounding heathenism: but these ceased in time to correspond to actual ethical and theological needs.

Accordingly, if it was to continue to be the authentic law of God, the Mosaic Law had to undergo certain developments. These developments do not change the essential content of the Law—on the contrary, they safeguard its divine substance, by transposing and adapting it to the requirements of new circumstances and new times. It follows that certain precepts of the Law have now fallen into desuetude.

Judaism itself felt the need for this development, for the *Halakah* is nothing but an interpretation of the written Law in view of new conditions. But with the Jews, development has consisted of constant augmentation of the Torah, without at the same time sweeping away the dead leaves that are no longer of use to the living tree.

SCHISM

The extension of salvation to the nations could in principle have come about in either of two ways. Firstly, it could have been by a natural development, by a growth, a steady spontaneous evolution, an expansion of the People of God, of such a kind that Israel would have wrought the inner transformation of all mankind, its slow but increasing and continuous spiritualization

and sanctification. Thus mankind, the whole *adam*, would have become Israel, as was promised to Abraham, that he should become a great people, and that all the races of the earth should find a blessing in him.

Such an expansion of Israel, finishing by God's people becoming co-extensive with the human race, would, we repeat, have involved a development: not simply an increase in numbers and in holiness, but also a recognition of the decrepitude of part of the Law; not simply a renewal, but also a corresponding consciousness of what was outworn. For the Mosaic Law, which had been the safeguard of Israel's earlier growth, was also a wall of separation between her and other peoples. The part played by the Law had in fact been ambivalent. It had protected Israel and kept her from the corruption of her neighbours, it had enabled her to become a 'people of saints'; but it also became a source of antagonism, a hindrance to the extension of God's salvation to the Gentiles, a piece of armour that threatened to smother God's people and make them incapable of fulfilling their calling to universality.

Israel was at this critical point when Paul began his mission.

On the other hand, the extension of salvation could come about in a more drastic way, by a break in the children of God that would allow the substance of the knowledge of God to pass over to the Gentile nations, and enable them to enter this divine community. It was the way of rending apart and schism: instead of

Israel opening herself to that universality that is part of her essence and vocation, and tearing down the thorny hedge of ritual observances, she could refuse the development that God proposed to her. In that case, she would henceforth be divided: on the one hand, an Israel 'according to the flesh', the posterity of Abraham; on the other, an Israel open to all men, which takes over the vocation of universal Church and no less claims Abraham as father, in accord with the promise.

It was this second possibility that in fact took place.

In his *Essay on the Development of Christian Doctrine*, John Henry Newman analyses how schism comes about when man refuses to follow a development willed by God; and he declares that one of the causes of religious corruption is the refusal to recognize doctrinal evolution and an obstinate adherence to bygone ideas. The schism that divided the people of God illustrates this.

'The Church ... conscious of her historical and spiritual continuity with the faithful Israel of the Old Covenant, will never look on the Israel separated from her as an *alien* people; rather does she see that Israel as a *severed branch* of the people of God, whose standing still when the divine work was taking a decisive step forward was equivalent to schism.'* Christianity is a development into the fullness of the Law, and Israel refused to follow it, in the name of faithfulness to the Law. So Christianity is infidelity in the eyes of Judaism, because Christians regard certain commandments of the Law as superseded; and Judaism is infidelity in the eyes of the Church, because Judaism remains fixed at a stage of God's work which is overpast.

I am not deceiving you, I am telling you the truth in Christ's name, with the full assurance of a conscience enlightened by the Holy Spirit, when I tell you of the great sorrow, the continual anguish I feel in my heart, and how it has ever been my wish that I myself might be doomed to separation from Christ, if that would benefit my brethren, my own kinsmen by race. They are Israelites, adopted as God's sons; the visible presence, and the covenant, and the giving of the law, and the Temple

* P. Démann, *Israël et l'unité de l'Église* (Cahiers Sioniens, No. 1, 1953).

worship, and the promises, are their inheritance; the patriarchs belong to them, and theirs is the human stock from which Christ came; Christ, who rules as God over all things, blessed for ever, Amen. And yet it is not as if God's promise had failed of its effect. Not all those who are sprung from Israel are truly Israelites; not all the posterity of Abraham are Abraham's children. . . . (Rom. 9: 1–7)

Here St. Paul uses a dialectic that he uses again with reference to circumcision: Israel is defined by faithfulness to a divine call. There is, then, a false Israel, Israel only in appearance, and a true Israel, Israel according to the spirit, the Israel of God. Accordingly, one can belong to Israel according to the flesh without really sharing in the Israel of God, which is defined by its truth and fidelity to him.

Brethren, they have all the good will of my heart, all my prayers to God, for their salvation. That they are jealous for God's honour, I can testify; but it is with imperfect understanding. They did not recognize God's way of justification, and so they tried to institute a way of their own, instead of submitting to his. Christ has superseded the law, bringing justification to anyone who will believe. (Rom. 10: 1–4)

Tell me, then, has God disowned his people? That is not to be thought of. Why, I am an Israelite myself, descended from Abraham; Benjamin is my tribe. No, God has not disowned the people which, from the first, he recognized as his. Do you not remember what scripture tells us about Elias? The complaint, I mean, which he made before God about Israel; 'Lord, they have killed thy prophets, and overthrown thy altars; I am the only one left, and my life, too, is threatened.' And what does the divine revelation tell him? There are seven thousand men I have kept true to myself, with knees that never bowed to Baal. So it is in our time; a remnant has remained true; grace has chosen it. . . .

The result of their false step has been to bring the Gentiles salvation. . . . Why then, if their false step has enriched the world, if the Gentiles have been enriched by their default, what must we expect when it is made good? (I am speaking now to you Gentiles.) As long as my apostolate is to the Gentiles, I mean to make much of my office, in the hope of stirring up my own flesh and blood to emulation, and saving some of them. If the losing of them has meant a world reconciled to God, what can the winning of them mean, but life risen from the dead?

When the first loaf is consecrated, the whole batch is consecrated with it; so, when the root is consecrated, the branches are consecrated too. The branches have been thinned out, and thou, a wild olive, hast been grafted in among them; sharest, with them, the root and the richness of the true olive. That is no reason why thou shouldst boast thyself better than the branches; remember, in thy mood of boastfulness, that thou owest life to the root, not the root to thee. Branches were cut away, thou wilt tell me, so that I might be grafted in. True enough, but it was for want of faith that they were cut away, and it is only faith that keeps thee where thou art; thou hast no reason for pride, rather for fear; God was unforgiving with the branches that were native to the tree, what if he should find occasion to be unforgiving with thee too?

There is graciousness, then, in God, and there is also severity. His severity is for those who have fallen away, his graciousness is for thee, only so long as thou dost continue in his grace; if not, thou too shalt be pruned away. Just so they too will be grafted in, if they do not continue in their unbelief; to graft them in afresh is not beyond God's power. Indeed, it was against nature when thou wast grafted on to the true olive's stock, thou, who wert native to the wild olive; it will be all the easier for him to graft these natural branches on to their own parent stock.

I must not fail, brethren, to make this revelation known to you; or else you might have too good a conceit of yourselves. Blindness has fallen upon a part of Israel, but only until the tale of the Gentile nations is complete; then the whole of Israel will find salvation, as we read in scripture, 'A deliverer shall come from Sion, to rid Jacob of his unfaithfulness; and this shall be the fulfilment of my covenant with them, when I take away their sins.' In the preaching of the gospel, God rejects them, to make room for you; but in his elective purpose he still welcomes them, for the sake of their fathers; God does not repent of the gifts he makes, or of the calls he issues. (Rom. 11: 1–5, 11–29)

Paul's starting-point in these passages is his own living experience: Israel as a whole did not welcome the word that God had spoken to her, and it was after this refusal that Paul turned to take the Gospel to the heathen gentiles. Only a minority of the Jews believed the Good News, while Gentiles flocked into the Church. The Synagogue's refusal worked out to the advantage of the heathen. But there was more to it than that. Had Israel accepted Christ without at the same time pulling down the hedge of the Law's ritual precepts and observances, there would have been, instead of the universal Church, a Judaeo-Christian church; and this would have effectually excluded the Gentiles from God's people, for heathen nations would never have put themselves under the yoke of the Law.

This was a vital matter for the Church, a real crisis, a revolution, the throes of birth; and Paul was the midwife who broke the umbilical cord by which the Church was attached to Judaism. Instead of growing by a continuous process, the people of God was enlarged dialectically, by Israel's refusal and the coming in of the Gentiles. But the schism is not definitive. When all the nations are numbered among the covenanted people, then shall the whole of Israel be saved.

Jerusalem

THE JERUSALEM CONFERENCE
(in the year 49 or 50)

St. Paul was the theorist of this dialectic. The mission had
begun before him, and the Church, through her missionaries,
had spontaneously broken through the barrier of observances.
But it was Paul who provided the theoretical justification for so
doing; it was he who undertook the contest with both Judaism
and Judaeo-Christians that enabled the Church to be fully born
and to be born free. In several of his letters and in the book of
Acts there is information about these difficulties.

But now some visitors came down from Judaea, who began
to tell the brethren, 'You cannot be saved without being circumcised according to the tradition of Moses.' Paul and Barnabas were drawn into a great controversy with them; and it was
decided that Paul and Barnabas and certain of the rest should

go up to see the apostles and presbyters in Jerusalem about this question. So the church saw them on their way, and they passed through Phoenice and Samaria, relating how the Gentiles were turning to God, and so brought great rejoicing to all the brethren.

When they reached Jerusalem, they were welcomed by the church, and by the apostles and presbyters; and they told them of all that God had done to aid them. But some believers who belonged to the party of the Pharisees came forward and declared, 'They must be circumcised; we must call upon them to keep the law of Moses.'

When the apostles and presbyters assembled to decide about this matter, there was much disputing over it, until Peter rose and said to them, 'Brethren, you know well enough how from early days it has been God's choice that the Gentiles should hear the message of the gospel from my lips, and so learn to believe. God, who can read men's hearts, has assured them of his favour by giving the Holy Spirit to them as to us. He would not make any difference between us and them; he had removed all the uncleanness from their hearts when he gave them faith. How is it, then, that you would now call God in question, by putting a yoke on the necks of the disciples, such as we and our fathers have been too weak to bear? It is by the grace of our Lord Jesus Christ that we hoped to be saved, and they no less.'

Then the whole company kept silence, and listened to Barnabas and Paul describing all the signs and wonders God had performed among the Gentiles by their means . . .

Thereupon it was resolved by the apostles and presbyters, with the agreement of the whole church, to choose out some of their own number and despatch them to Antioch with Paul and Barnabas; namely, Judas who was called Barsabas, and Silas, who were leading men among the brethren. And they sent, by their hands, this message in writing:

'To the Gentile brethren in Antioch, Syria and Cilicia, their brethren the apostles and presbyters send greeting. We hear that some of our number who visited you have disquieted you by what they said, unsettling your consciences, although we had given them no such commission; and therefore, meeting together with common purpose of heart, we have resolved to send you chosen messengers, in company with our well-beloved Barnabas and Paul, men who have staked their lives for the name of our Lord Jesus Christ. We have given this commission to Judas and Silas, who will confirm the message by word of mouth. It is the Holy Spirit's pleasure and ours that no burden should be laid upon you beyond these, which cannot be avoided; you are to abstain from what is sacrificed to idols, from blood-meat and meat which has been strangled, and from fornication. If you keep away from such things, you will have done your part. Farewell.'

So they took their leave and went down to Antioch, where they called the multitude together and delivered the letter to them; and they, upon reading it, were rejoiced at this encouragement. Judas and Silas, for they were prophets too, said much to encourage the brethren and establish their faith; they stayed there for some time before the brethren let them go home, in peace, to those who had sent them. But Silas had a mind to remain there; so Judas went back alone to Jerusalem. Paul and Barnabas waited at Antioch, teaching and preaching God's word, with many others to help them. (Acts 15: 1–12, 22–35)

In the letter to the Galatians there is a passage about a visit of Paul to Jerusalem, which probably relates to this conference, and it also tells us about his remonstrance with St. Peter at Antioch later on.

Then, after an interval of fourteen years, once again I went up to Jerusalem with Barnabas; and Titus also accompanied me. I went up in obedience to a revelation, and there I communicated to them (only in private, to men of repute) the gospel I always preach among the Gentiles; was it possible that the course I had taken and was taking was useless?

And it is not even true to say that they insisted on my companion Titus, who was a Greek, being circumcised; we were only thinking of those false brethren who had insinuated themselves into our company so as to spy on the liberty which we enjoy in Christ Jesus, meaning to make slaves of us. To these we did not give ground for a moment by way of obedience; we were resolved that the true principles of the gospel should remain undisturbed in your possession. But as for what I owe to those who were of some repute—it matters little to me who or what they were, God makes no distinction between man and man—these men of repute, I say, had nothing to communicate

'When Cephas came to Antioch, I opposed him openly'
Gal. 2: 11. (Peter and Paul; 4th–5th century,
Aquileia Museum)

to me. On the contrary, those who were reputed to be the main support of the Church, James and Cephas and John, saw plainly that I was commissioned to preach to the uncircumcised, as Peter was to the circumcised; he whose power had enabled Peter to become the apostle of the circumcised, had enabled me to become the apostle of the Gentiles. And so, recognizing the grace God had given me, they joined their right hands in fellowship with Barnabas and myself; the Gentiles were to be our province, the circumcised theirs. Only we were to remember the poor; which was the very thing I had set myself to do.

Afterwards, when Cephas came to Antioch, I opposed him openly; he stood self-condemned. He had been eating with the Gentiles, until we were visited by certain delegates from James; but when these came, he began to draw back and hold himself aloof, overawed by the supporters of circumcision. The rest of the Jews were no less false to their principles; Barnabas himself was carried away by their insincerity.

So, when I found that they were not following the true path of the gospel, I said to Cephas in front of them all, 'Since thou, who art a born Jew, dost follow the Gentile, not the Jewish way of life, by what right dost thou bind the Gentiles to live like Jews?' (Gal. 2: 1–14)

The Church of the Circumcision and the Church of the Gentiles (5th century, Santa Sabina, Rome)

CIRCUMCISION

Circumcision was historically the mark of fellowship in the people of God. This outward sign of the Covenant is henceforward superfluous; but the reality that it signifies still remains. The outward sign has not only ceased to be useful: it has become a stumbling-block, holding back the Gentiles and so preventing the fullness of God's people. What had had a necessary positive function in the formation of that people is seen now to be a negative element, standing in the way of the carrying out of God's purpose.

Circumcision then is continued, but inwardly. Its substance is kept, fellowship with the Lord in spirit, but the mark of this in the flesh is done away with. 'There is no virtue either in circumcision or in the want of it; it is keeping the commandments of

God that signifies' (1 Cor. 7: 19); 'Once we are in Christ, circumcision means nothing, and the want of it means nothing; the faith that finds its expression in love is all that matters . . . there has been a new creation' (Gal. 5: 6, 6: 15).

It is in this way that Paul can call the Church 'God's true Israel' (Gal. 6: 16); not that the previous Israel was not also God's true Israel, but because the Church had in fact already begun with Abraham, the faithful Israel of the holy men and prophets of the Old Covenant was already the Church. Onward from Abraham, the father of them that believe, there is one people of God, but a part of them are faithless, whether in the Hebrew Israel or in the Church today; in the one as in the other there are those 'who falsely claim to be Jews when they are none' (Apoc. 3: 9; cf. 2: 9). There is a pseudo-Israel, pseudo-Jews and then pseudo-Christians, who observe outward forms but are wanting in spirit and in truth.

Paul distinguishes the Israel of God from the Israel 'according to the flesh', circumcision in spirit from bodily circumcision: 'Circumcision, to be sure, is of value, so long as thou keepest the law; but if thou breakest the law, thy circumcision has lost its effect. And if one who has never been circumcised observes the conditions of the law, does it not follow that he, though uncircumcised, will be reckoned as one who is circumcised? That he, who keeps the law, though uncircumcised in body, will be able to pass judgement on thee, who breakest the law, though circumcised according to the letter of it? To be a Jew is not to be a Jew outwardly; to be circumcised is not to be circumcised outwardly, in the flesh. He is a Jew indeed who is one inwardly; true circumcision is achieved in the heart, according to the spirit, not the letter of the law, for God's, not for man's approval' (Rom. 2: 25–29).

Here Paul is carrying on the idea expressed in Leviticus (26: 41), '. . . until those defiled [literally, 'uncircumcised'] hearts learn to be ashamed . . .'; in Deuteronomy (10:16, 30: 6), '. . . rid your hearts of defilement [literally, 'circumcise your hearts'], a stiff-necked people no longer'; 'He will rid thy heart, and the hearts of thy children, of all defilement, and thou wilt find life in loving the Lord thy God, heart and soul'; and by Jeremiah (4: 4); 'You must be circumcised afresh . . . of heart's defilement rid yourselves.'

Once again, St. Paul justified in theory what the Church had already done in practice at her sudden extension (the theoretical advocates of some big change are often simply giving voice to an actual widespread movement). In the face of Judaism and the Judaeo-Christians, he declared that the 'letter' of circumcision, as a bodily rite, was no longer necessary to membership in the people of God. This development of the Mosaic Law was justified because the times were no longer the same: the Christ, the Fulfilment, had come. In Christ, 'you have been circumcised with a circumcision that was not man's handiwork' (Col. 2: 11).

> As for circumcision, it is we who practise it, we who serve God with the spirit, and take pride in Christ Jesus, instead of putting our trust in outward observances. Not that I have no outward claims to give me confidence; if others put their trust in outward claims, I can do so with better reason. I was circumcised seven days after I was born; I come from the stock of Israel, from the tribe of Benjamin, Hebrew-speaking as my parents were before me. Over the law, I was a Pharisee; to prove my loyalty, I persecuted the Church of God; in observing what the law commands, I was beyond reproach. And all this, which once stood to my credit, I now write down as loss, for the love of Christ.
>
> For that matter, there is nothing I do not write down as loss compared with the high privilege of knowing Christ Jesus, my Lord; for love of him I have lost everything, treat everything else as refuse, if I may have Christ to my credit. In him I would render my account, not claiming any justification that is my own work, given me by the law, but the justification that comes from believing in Jesus Christ, God's gift on condition of our faith. Him I would learn to know, and the virtue of his resurrection, and what it means to share his sufferings, moulded into the pattern of his death, in the hope of achieving resurrection from the dead. (Phil. 3: 3-11)

*The Law and the Prophets bear witness to God's
way of justification Rom. 3: 21.
(La-Charité-sur-Loire)*

JUSTICE THROUGH FAITH

Justice in the Old Testament (*sedaka*) and in St. Paul (*dikaiosune*) has not the wholly juridical and moral sense that we give to the term nowadays.* The signification of 'justice' in the Bible is above all metaphysical or, more exactly, theologic: it is the total transformation of man by which he becomes like to God and fit to share in the divine life. In the Bible, justice before God is what we now call holiness: conformity with the will and very being of God—'Keep yourselves apart and be a holy people; remember what God you worship' (Lev. 20: 7). Justice, therefore, is no external legality, imputed by observance of the Law or by God's decree. It is something imprinted in man's being, involving his entire renewal.

This integral transformation which enables a man to be called 'just' is the work of God through his Spirit. Man cannot attain holiness by his own sufficiency, for holiness is a relationship of friendship, an existential relationship wherein God gives that newness of heart that is called justice: 'it is the gift of God'.

---

* The words *sedaka, dikaiosune, justitia* have often been rendered in English as 'righteousness'; this word too has come to have a predominantly moral connotation.

Justice then cannot be attained by any practice or observance: it is life, and God alone can give the supernatural life of holiness. Adherence to the Law of Moses was necessary for the making of a people holy and the Israel of God, it was a necessary condition of belonging to that people, but by itself it was not enough. Only God can transform the being he has created and make him like Himself, that is, make him holy, 'just'.

The value of the Law must not be minimized, nor the attitude of its faithful doctors caricatured, as is so often done. The Law was not an empty formalism: it was an authentic instrument of God's work. It did not require external conformity to the code alone, it also called for an inward, spiritual condition, a change of heart, for love of God and love of one's neighbour; as well as physical circumcision, it was concerned for spiritual circumcision, of the heart.

But it was beyond the power of the Law by itself to bring about this newness of heart, this holiness, at which it aimed. Only God, who 'trieth the hearts and reins', can do this work of new creation: I will give you a new heart, and breathe a new spirit into you.' The Law was like a stick by means of which a plant grows straight, but the spark of life must first be in the plant. 'If a law had been given that was capable of *imparting life* to us, it would have been for the law to bring us justification' (Gal. 3: 21).

The Law was necessary, but it was not enough; its covenant had to be completed by another, a new covenant, one no longer of judgement but of life. Such was the mind of the prophets: 'A time is coming, the Lord says, when I mean to ratify a new covenant with the people of Israel and with the people of Juda. It will not be like the covenant which I made with their fathers, on the day when I took them by the hand, to rescue them from Egypt; that they should break my covenant, and I, all the while, their master, the Lord says. No, this is the covenant I will grant the people of Israel, the Lord says, when that time comes. I will implant my law in their innermost thoughts, engrave it in their hearts; I will be their God, and they shall be my people. There will be no need for neighbour to teach neighbour, or brother to teach brother, the knowledge of the Lord; all will know me, from the highest to the lowest . . .' (Jer. 31: 31–34). 'I will give you a new heart, and breathe a new spirit into you; I will take away from your breasts those hearts that are hard as stone, and give you human hearts instead. I will make my spirit penetrate you . . .' (Ezech. 36: 25–27).

It is this limitation of the Old Law, its powerlessness to obtain holiness, that St. Paul points to when he declares that justification cannot be obtained by observance of the Law and that only faith in Christ can justify us. 'There was something the law could not do, because flesh and blood could not lend it the power; and this God has done, by sending us his own Son, in the fashion of our guilty nature' (Rom. 8: 3).

The Law's function was to show the sinfulness of sin and to give it its name, so that men might reject it. In this sense, its function was a negative one, and it was expressed in negative terms: 'Thou shalt not . . .' It made men conscious of the old sinfulness that was present in them from the days of Adam, and caused them to react from it—but it could not make them holy. Only God could do that, transforming and renewing their hearts by his Spirit. 'No human creature can become acceptable in his sight by observing the law; what the law does is to give us the full consciousness of sin' (Rom. 3: 20). Holiness, 'justice', 'justification', is wrought by God's grace:

But, in these days, God's way of justification has at last been brought to light; one which was attested by the law and the prophets, but stands apart from the law; God's way of justification through faith in Jesus Christ, meant for everybody and sent down upon everybody without distinction, if he has faith. All alike have sinned, all alike are unworthy of God's praise. And justification comes to us as a free gift from his grace, through our redemption in Christ Jesus. . . .

What has become, then, of thy pride? No room has been left for it. On what principle? The principle which depends on observances? No, the principle which depends on faith; our contention is, that a man is justified by faith apart from the observances of the law.

Is God the God of the Jews only? Is he not the God of the

Gentiles too? Of the Gentiles too assuredly; there is only one God, who will justify the circumcised man if he learns to believe, and the Gentile because he believes. Does that mean that we are using faith to rob the law of its force? No, we are setting the law on its right footing. (Rom. 3: 21-24, 27-31.)

We are Jews by right of nature, we do not come from the guilty stock of the Gentiles; yet we found out that it is through faith in Jesus Christ, not by obeying the law, that a man is justified. We, like anyone else, had to learn to believe in Jesus Christ, so that we might be justified by faith in Christ, not by observance of the law. Observance of the law cannot win acceptance for a single human creature. (Gal. 2: 15-16.)

How is faith able to 'justify' us? It is by the indwelling of God's holy Spirit in us, which makes us a new creature, transforms and sanctifies us. Faith *is* holiness, it *is* God's justice; it is the Spirit abiding in our new heart, in our inwardness. Through faith in Christ we become a new man; Christ justifies us, Christ sanctifies us, if we share in his life by faith. 'When God sent his Son into the world, it was not to reject the world, but so that the world might find salvation through him. For the man who believes in him, there is no rejection; the man who does not believe is already rejected; he has not found faith in the name of God's only-begotten Son. Rejection lies in this, that when the light came into the world men preferred darkness to light; preferred it, because their doings were evil' (John 3: 7-19).

Faith is the supernatural understanding of himself and of the mystery of his work that God bestows on us. When grace is offered and we freely consent to it, then this understanding through the Holy Spirit becomes ours. In this sense, faith is the sign of the depth of our good will: it shows that we have accepted God's supernatural friendship and that we choose him rather than falsehood and nothingness. Faith is the sign of our justness, because it shows that the Holy Spirit who sanctifies abides in us. That is why Peter can say that God has purified hearts by faith (Acts 15: 9). Faith *manifests* purity of heart in that it shows us freely consenting to life in God; it *brings about* that purity by setting us free from our own deceitful illusions. The fact is that our freedom is made real only in and through faith, that faith which, as St. John says, is our victory over the 'world'. By faith it is that we become children of God and joint-heirs with Christ; faith is supernatural life in us, a participation in the life of the Trinity.

A passage in St. Peter's second letter (3: 14–16) is very much to the point in relation to this part of the Epistle to the Romans: 'Beloved . . . , if our Lord stays his hand, count it part of his mercy. Our beloved brother Paul, with the wisdom God has granted him, has written you a letter, in which, as in all his letters, he talks of this. (Though indeed, there are passages in them difficult to understand, and these, like the rest of scripture, are twisted into a wrong sense by ignorant and restless minds, to their own undoing.)' Nevertheless, Paul's thought is clear once we have grasped the meaning of his ideas in their biblical setting (the fundamental character of his thought and language is essentially that of the Old Testament); when, too, we have rid his thought of the burdens that scholastics (notably Lutheran scholastics) have imposed on his words.

That the Law is powerless to justify us does not, of course, mean that we are free to disregard its spiritual and timeless element. The part of it that Paul and Christianity regard as abolished is the ritual part, the observances that no longer have any historical and prophetical meaning. The substance of the Law remains ('one jot or one flourish shall not disappear from the law'), and its substance is the commandment of holiness. 'And if it is grace, not the law, we serve, are we therefore to fall into sin? God forbid. . . . Thus you escaped from the bondage of sin, and became the slaves of right-doing instead' (Rom. 6: 15, 18); 'We have died, once for all, to sin; can we breathe its air again?' (Rom. 6: 2).

When Paul writes that man is justified without the works of the Law, he means, firstly, that justness does not come from the observance of the Law but from God; and, secondly, that God now sanctifies us without our being bound by Judaic ritual—circumcision, forbidden foods, and the rest. But the whole *essence* of the Law still holds, and moreover, Christ has given it its fullness. The Ten Commandments are not done away with;

on the contrary, the Beatitudes complete and fill them out in all their stringency: 'If your justice does not give fuller measure than the justice of the scribes and Pharisees . . .' (Matt. 5: 20).

That man is justified by faith, without the works of the Law, does not mean that he does not have to live his faith and carry it out in actual circumstances: 'The kingdom of heaven will not give entrance to every man who calls me Master, Master; only to the man that does the will of my Father who is in heaven' (Matt. 7: 21). Faith cannot be dissociated from exercising it in actuality. So far from excluding charity, holiness born of faith implies and begets it: '. . . faith that finds its expression in love' (Gal. 5: 6). The justice which comes of faith bears fruit in the works of love that the Lord commands.

The Epistle of James is directed against a sophistical interpretation of Paul's mind which represents 'works' as being, not, as with Paul, observance of Judaic precepts, but living according to the Lord's commandments of love: 'Of what use is it, my brethren, if a man claims to have faith, and has no deeds to show for it? Can faith save him then? Here is a brother, here is a sister, going naked, left without the means to secure their daily food; if one of you says to them, "Go in peace, warm yourselves and take your fill", without providing for their bodily needs, of what use is it? Thus faith, if it has no deeds to shew for itself, has lost its own principle of life. We shall be inclined to say to him, "Thou hast faith, but I have deeds to show". Shew me this faith of thine without any deeds to prove it, and I am prepared, by my deeds, to prove my own faith. Thou believest that there is only one God; that is well enough, but then, so do the devils, and the devils shrink from him in terror' (Jas. 2: 14–19).

Only a crooked mind can find any opposition between James's thought and Paul's. They use the same word, 'works', but they are not talking about the same thing.

Put into modern terms, Paul is saying something like this: What Christianity calls holiness—a supernatural life through the Spirit of God—cannot be attained at the ethical or ritual level: observance neither of the moral law nor of religious rites is sufficient to make saints of us. It is possible for a man to be integrally 'moral' and yet not have a grain of holiness in him, because holiness implies the supernatural, theologic, virtues—faith, hope, charity. Furthermore, an 'ethical' man often displays a certain imperviousness to grace, to supernatural life; as Péguy put it, he is not porous to grace (*il ne 'mouille' pas à la grâce*): he is too content with his own virtue to feel any desire for a holiness that comes from God. But holiness is not virtue— ✓ it is life in God and of God. On the other hand, a man who is ethically unsatisfactory is often better disposed towards grace, more open to the coming of Christ, through the very rent that sin has made: 'The publicans and the harlots are further on the road to God's kingdom than you', you, the chief priests and elders of the people, doctors of the Law. The only person to whom Jesus promised salvation was the thief crucified beside him: 'This day thou shalt be with me in Paradise.'

In the language of Kierkegaard, holiness is not found at the 'ethical stage' but at the 'religious stage'. A man may live his ✓ life in the fullest conformity with the rules of ethics, and yet be totally wanting in holiness. St. Paul says so in the course of a famous passage that we shall have to come back to: 'I may give away all that I have to feed the poor; I may give myself up to be burnt at the stake; if I lack charity, it goes for nothing.'

Immanuel Kant tried to reduce 'justice' from the Christian supernatural level to the ethical level, and his *Critique of Practical Reason* is an endeavour analogous to that which Paul had to fight against among the Galatians, namely, to look for justice in the observance of a moral law. All such attempts as these are due to a neglect of the meaning of supernatural life, the life of 'dialogue' and exchange between the Spirit of God, his grace, and ourselves.

If we can be justified through the law, then Christ's death was needless.

Senseless Galatians, who is it that has cast a spell on you, that you should refuse your loyalty to the truth, you, before whom Jesus Christ has been exposed to view on his cross? Let me be content with asking you one question, Was it from observance of the law that the Spirit came to you, or from obeying the call of faith? Are you so far out of your right senses? You dedicated your first beginnings to the Spirit; and can you now find your completion in outward things? Was it to no purpose that you went through so much? Since it seems it was to no purpose. When God lavishes his Spirit on you and enables you to perform miracles, what is the reason for it? Your observance of the law, or your obedience to the call of faith? Remember how Abraham put his faith in God, and it was reckoned virtue in him.

You must recognize, then, that Abraham's real children are the children of his faith. There is a passage in scripture which, long beforehand, brings to Abraham the good news, 'Through thee all the nations shall be blessed; and that passage looks forward to God's justification of the Gentiles by faith . . . It is those, then, who take their stand on faith that share the blessing Abraham's faithfulness won.' (Gal. 2: 21; 3: 1–9.)

The word of Paul is your warrant for this; if you are for being circumcised, Christ is of no value to you at all. (Gal. 5: 2.)

So that the law was our tutor, bringing us to Christ, to find in faith our justification. When faith comes, then we are no longer under the rule of a tutor; through faith in Christ Jesus

The Publican and the Pharisee Luke 18: 10–14. (*6th century, Ravenna*)

*Paul and Peter pray for the world enslaved to
'deities who were in truth no deities at all'
Gal. 4: 8. (Vezelay)*

you are all now God's sons. All you who have been baptized
in Christ's name have put on the person of Christ; no more Jew
or Gentile, no more slave and freeman, no more male and fe-
male; you are all one person in Jesus Christ. And if you belong
to Christ, then you are indeed Abraham's children; the promised
inheritance is yours. (Gal. 3: 24–29.)

THE HEATHEN

When he formed a people for the work of man's salvation,
God set up a dialectic between this people and the rest of mankind, 'the nations'.

The Law, which was the mould of the Chosen People and

protected its growth, became in man's hands a wall of separation between God's people and the rest of mankind. With the coming of Christ, who is the fullness of the Law, the ritual barrier was thrown down; the nations entered into the people of God, and Israel became the universal Church. In Christ Jesus there is no longer Jew and Greek, man and woman, slave and free, for Christ is all in all. It is through him that the wall dividing mankind into two parts is destroyed, by the abolition of the Law of precepts with its ordinances.

What, before Christ's coming, was the state of the heathen nations that were outside the *phyle* of revelation and salvation? In several places of his letters St. Paul describes the condition of man without God, without knowledge of the living God.

> Formerly you had no knowledge of God; you lived as the slaves of deities who were in truth no deities at all. Now you have recognized the true God, or rather, the true God has recognized you. (Gal. 4: 8, 9.)
>
> This, then, is my message to you: I call upon you in the Lord's name not to live like the Gentiles, who make vain fancies their rule of their life. Their minds are clouded with darkness; the hardness of their hearts breeds in them an ignorance, which estranges them from the divine life. (Eph. 4: 17–18.)
>
> He found you dead men; such were your transgressions, such were the sinful ways you lived in. That was when you followed the fashion of this world, when you owned a prince whose domain is in the lower air, that spirit whose influence is still at work among the unbelievers. We too, all of us, were once of their company; our life was bounded by natural appetites, and we did what corrupt nature or our own calculation would have us do, with God's displeasure for our birthright, like other men.
>
> How rich God is in mercy, with what an excess of love he loved us! Our sins had made dead men of us, and he, in giving life to Christ, gave life to us too; it is his grace that has saved you; raised us up too, enthroned us too above the heavens, in Christ Jesus. He would have all future ages see, in that clemency which he shewed us in Christ Jesus, the surpassing richness of his grace. Yes, it was grace that saved you, with faith for its instrument; it did not come from yourselves, it was God's gift, not from any action of yours, or there would be room for

pride. No, we are his design; God has created us in Christ Jesus, pledged to such good actions as he has prepared beforehand, to be the employment of our lives.

Remember, then, what you once were, the Gentiles, according to all outward reckoning; those who claim an outward circumcision which is man's handiwork call you the uncircumcised. In those days there was no Christ for you; you were outlaws from the commonwealth of Israel, strangers to every covenant, with no promise to hope for, with the world about you, and no God.

But now you are in Christ Jesus; now, through the blood of Christ, you have been brought close, you who were once so far away. He is our bond of peace; he has made the two nations one, breaking down the wall that was a barrier between us, the enmity there was between us, in his own mortal nature. He has put an end to the law with its decrees, so as to make peace, remaking the two human creatures as one in himself; both sides, united in a single body, he would reconcile to God through his cross, inflicting death, in his own person, upon the feud. So he came, and his message was of peace for you who were far off, peace for those who were near; far off or near, united in the the same Spirit, we have access through him to the Father.

You are no longer exiles, then, or aliens; the saints are your fellow-citizens, you belong to God's household. Apostles and prophets are the foundation on which you were built, and the chief corner-stone of it is Jesus Christ himself. In him the whole fabric is bound together, as it grows into a temple, dedicated to the Lord; in him you too are being built in with the rest, so that God may find in you a dwelling-place for his Spirit. (Eph. 2.)

God, then, in those times left all peoples to walk in their own ways; 'yet even so he has not left us without some proof of what he is; it is his bounty that grants us rain from heaven, and the seasons which give birth to our crops, so that we have nourishment and comfort to our heart's desire' (Acts 14: 16).

This failure of the nations to recognize God for centuries on end was not normal, that is, it was not the ignorance of a still young mankind who had been given no means of knowing him. It was the ignorance of ageing peoples who had turned away from

God and his holiness, who had corrupted their ways, as the Bible says. 'God's anger is being revealed from heaven: his anger against the impiety and wrong-doing of the men whose wrong-doing denies his truth its full scope. The knowledge of God is clear to their minds; God himself has made it clear to them; from the foundations of the world men have caught sight of his invisible nature, his eternal power and his divineness, as they are known through his creatures. Thus there is no excuse for them; although they had the knowledge of God, they did not honour him or give thanks to him as God; they became fantastic in their notions, and their senseless hearts grew benighted . . .' (Rom. 1: 18–21).

Always has it been taught in the Church that God is knowable from his creation, and St. Paul here takes up a theme that is equally constant in the Bible: understanding appertains to man's will and his freedom. The contrary of understanding is not mis-understanding or error; it is man's sin when he refuses to see something which he would be able to see did he not prefer dark-ness to light; as it is said in the Gospel of John (3: 19), 'men preferred darkness to light; preferred it, because their doings were evil'.

It follows that not to understand—what the prophets call 'foolishness'—is the fundamental sin, sin against the spirit, *the* sin. Foolishness comes from a choice made in the secrecy of the heart; man's heart is darkened by his own hidden will. 'They, who claimed to be so wise, turned fools, and exchanged the glory of the imperishable God for representations of perishable man, of bird and beast and reptile' (Rom. 1: 22-23). Idolatry is the basal foolishness, as the prophets taught: metaphysical foolish-ness that confounds God the Creator with creatures that perish.

The foolishness that comes from the heart's choosing is re-flected in man's behaviour.

That is why God abandoned their lustful hearts to filthy practices of dishonouring their own bodies among themselves. They had exchanged God's truth for a lie, reverencing and wor-shipping the creature in preference to the Creator (blessed is he for ever, Amen); and, in return, God abandoned them to passions which brought dishonour to themselves. Their women exchanged natural for unnatural intercourse; and the men, on their side, giving up natural intercourse with women, were burnt up with desire for each other; men practising vileness with their fellow-men. Thus they have received a fitting retribution for their false belief.

And as they scorned to keep God in their view, so God has abandoned them to a frame of mind worthy of all scorn, that prompts them to disgraceful acts. They are versed in every kind of injustice, knavery, impurity, avarice, and ill-will; spiteful, murderous, contentious, deceitful, depraved, backbiters, slanderers, God's enemies; insolent, haughty, vainglorious; inventive in wickedness, disobedient to their parents; without prudence, without honour, without love, without loyalty, without pity. (Rom. 1: 24-31.)

So, after the fruitless attempt upon the Synagogue, Paul and his companions turned to the heathen nations, going amongst them to proclaim the Word of God who has come down amongst us, whom our hands have touched, whom our eyes have seen.

SECOND MISSIONARY JOURNEY
(from 49 or 50 to 52 or 53)

St. Paul's second missionary journey is narrated in the book
of the Acts of the Apostles.

After some days, Paul said to Barnabas, 'Let us go back and
visit the brethren in all the cities where we have preached the
word of the Lord, to see how they are doing.' And Barnabas
was for taking John, also called Mark, with them. But Paul
said, here was a man who left them when they reached Pamphylia, and took no part with them in the work; it was not right
to admit such a man to their company. So sharp was their disagreement, that they separated from each other; Barnabas took
Mark with him, and sailed off to Cyprus, while Paul chose Silas
for his companion and went on his journey, commended by the
brethren to the Lord's grace. And he travelled all through Syria
and Cilicia, establishing the churches in the faith . . .

So he reached Derbe, and Lystra. Here he met a disciple,
named Timothy, son of a believer who was a Jewess and a
Gentile father. He was well spoken of by the brethren at Lystra
and Iconium, and Paul resolved to take him as a companion on
his journey. But he was careful to circumcise him; he was
thinking of the Jews living in those parts, who all knew that
Timothy's father was a Gentile. As they passed from city to
city, they recommended to their observance the decree laid
down by the apostles and presbyters at Jerusalem. They found
the churches firmly established in the faith, and their numbers
daily increasing.

Thus they passed through Phrygia and the Galatian country;
the Holy Spirit prevented them from preaching the word
in Asia. Then, when they had come as far as Mysia on their
journey, they planned to enter Bithynia; but the Spirit of
Jesus would not allow it. So they crossed Mysia, and went down
to the sea at Troas.

Here Paul saw a vision in the night; a certain Macedonian
stood by him in entreaty, and said, 'Come over into Macedonia,
and help us.' That vision once seen, we were eager to sail for
Macedonia; we concluded that God had called us there to preach
to them. (Acts 15: 36 to 16: 10.)

After the tenth verse of chapter 16, just
quoted, the reader will notice that the
narrative changes from the third to the
first person: the writer, Luke the physician, now joins Paul and shares his travels
and labours.

> So we put out from Troas, made a
> straight course to Samothrace, and next
> day to Neapolis. Thence we reached
> Philippi, which is a Roman colony and
> the chief city in that part of Macedonia;
> in this city we remained for some days,
> conferring together.

On the sabbath day we went out beyond the city gates, by the river side, a
meeting-place, we were told, for prayer; and we sat down and
preached to the women who had assembled there. One of
those who were listening was a woman called Lydia, a purple-
seller from the city of Thyatira, and a worshipper of the true
God; and the Lord opened her heart, so that she was attentive
to Paul's preaching. She was baptized, with all her household;
and she was urgent with us; 'Now that you have decided that I
have faith in the Lord,' she said, 'come to my house and lodge
there'; and she would take no denial. (Acts 16: 11–15.)

At Philippi, Paul cast a pythonic, that is, divining, spirit out
of a young woman; whereupon her masters, who had made a
good thing out of her soothsaying, brought Paul and Silas before
the magistrates. 'These men, Jews by origin', they said, 'are
disturbing the peace of our city; they are recommending customs

Ruins of Philippi

which it is impossible for us, as Roman citizens, to admit or to observe.' The people clamoured indignantly, and the magistrates ordered Paul and Silas to be flogged and shut up in gaol. That night there was an earthquake, which brought about the conversion of the gaoler on the spot, and he took the two prisoners to his own house. The next day, after Paul had invoked his Roman citizenship, they were set free.

They continued their journey through Amphipolis and Appolonia, and so reached Thessalonica. Here the Jews had a synagogue, and Paul, as his custom was, paid them a visit there . . .

The Jews were indignant at this, and they found confederates among the riff-raff of the market-place, to make a disturbance and throw the city into an uproar . . .

Thereupon the brethren sent Paul and Silas away by night to Beroea . . .

But now some of the Thessalonian Jews, hearing that the word of God had been preached by Paul at Beroea too, came on there,

Athens: the Areopagus from the Acropolis

'To the unknown gods'
(*Altar found at Pergamos*)

ΘΕΟΙΣ ΑΓΝΩΣΤΟΙΣ
ΚΑΠΙΤ (ΩΝ)
ΔΑΔΟΥΚΟΣ

to upset and disturb the minds of the multitude; whereupon the brethren sent Paul away, to continue his journey up to the coast; Silas and Timothy remained there still. (Acts 17: 1–15.)

ATHENS:
THE WORD OF GOD AND THE PHILOSOPHERS

And while Paul was waiting for them in Athens, his heart was moved within him to find the city so much given over to idolatry, and he reasoned, not only in the synagogue with Jews and worshippers of the true God, but in the market-place, with all he met.

He encountered philosophers, Stoics and Epicureans, some of whom asked, 'What can his drift be, this dabbler?' While others said, 'He would appear to be proclaiming strange gods'; because he had preached to them about Jesus and the Resurrection. So they took him by the sleeve and led him up to the Areopagus; 'May we ask,' they said, 'what this new teaching is thou art delivering? Thou dost introduce terms which are strange to our ears; pray let us know what may be the meaning of it.' (No townsman of Athens, or stranger visiting it, has time for anything else than saying something new, or hearing it said.)

So Paul stood up in full view of the Areopagus, and said, 'Men of Athens, wherever I look I find you scrupulously

E

religious. Why, in examining your monuments as I passed by them, I found among others an altar which bore the inscription, TO THE UNKNOWN GOD. And it is this unknown object of your devotion that I am revealing to you.

'The God who made the world and all that is in it, that God who is Lord of heaven and earth, does not dwell in temples that our hands have made; no human handicraft can do him service, as if he stood in need of anything, he, who gives to all of us life and breath and all we have. It is he who has made, of one single stock, all the nations that were to dwell over the whole face of the earth. And he has given to each the cycles it was to pass through and the fixed limits of its habitation, leaving them to search for God; would they somehow grope their way towards him? Would they find him? And yet, after all, he is not far from any one of us; it is in him that we live, and move, and have our being; thus, some of your own poets have told us, for indeed, we are his children.

'Why then, if we are the children of God, we must not imagine that the divine nature can be represented in gold, or silver, or stone, carved by man's art and thought. God has shut his eyes to these passing follies of ours; now, he calls upon all men, everywhere, to repent, because he has fixed a day when he will pronounce just judgement on the whole world. And the man whom he has appointed for that end he has accredited to all of us, by raising him up from the dead.'

When resurrection from the dead was mentioned, some mocked, while others said, 'We must hear more from thee about this.' So Paul went away from among them. But there were men who attached themselves to him and learned to believe, among them Dionysius the Areopagite; and so did a woman called Damaris, and others with them. (Acts 17: 16–33.)

It is clear that Paul's meeting with the philosophers at Athens has a significance beyond that of the simple historical fact. It has a representative value: the confrontation of Jerusalem and Athens, of the wisdom of God expressed by the *nabhis* of Israel and the wisdom of men, of the theology of the living God which was made known to his beloved people and the theologies of paganism, idolatries, mystery religions, gnosticisms, of the metaphysic of the Bible and the metaphysic of the Gentiles.

When St. Paul proclaimed the Word in Jewish synagogues, he always began with the Scriptures. When he addressed pagans in Lycaonia (cf. Acts. 14: 16–17, quoted above) he appealed to their experience of pleasure as a point of entrance for the idea of a Bestower of all that is good.

At Athens, too, he looks for a stepping-stone, a piece of common ground, that he may express the teaching he wants to convey to these philosophers in language that they can understand. It is the missionary method. A man cannot recognize a truth unless, in some way and some measure, he is prepared for it and awaits it *from within.* In other words, no mission is possible, the evangelist cannot talk with effect, until God himself has been at work in the heart of the person addressed. Faith results from the convergence and meeting of these two 'testimonies': the expounded word of God, and the Spirit of God preparing and predisposing the understanding to welcome that word. No truth whatever can be conveyed to 'just anybody' at 'any old time': preparation is always necessary. For words of truth to be intelligible, they must *correspond* to some answering need and expectancy in the hearer.

Now Greek mythology was well peopled with divinities, but all the same this profusion of gods and goddesses does not seem to have satisfied the Greek soul: need was sometimes felt to dedicate altars to 'unknown gods'. This apparent unsatisfiedness, the gap that conjured up the possibility of an unknown god, was Paul's opportunity; he took it, and not without a certain irony. When he told the Athenians that they were very religious he was paying a compliment that was double-edged. For a Jew, their religiousness was precisely polytheism, idolatry—the abominable thing. From the pagan standpoint, a Jew was an atheist, precisely because he refused to worship the city's numerous gods. The Roman empire persecuted Jews as 'atheists'; we have only to recall the stupefaction of the victorious Roman soldiers when they broke into the Holy of holies of the Temple at Jerusalem: instead of the images that they expected, they found—*nothing*.

The Athenians' multitude of divinities made by their own minds and hands left them unsatisfied, and Paul, like the good missionary that he was, began there, with something already familiar that could bear fruit: 'It is this unknown object of your devotion whom I am revealing to you.' But there is no question of taking the line of least resistance. He went on to declare what in the circumstances was the most difficult point for his hearers to accept, one that was incompatible with the general structure of Greek philosophy and all pagan metaphysic: the Creation. 'The God who made the world and all that is in it. . . .'

By declaring, in the very heart of Athens, that God created the cosmos, St. Paul made a frontal attack on the fundamental principle of all the philosophy of antiquity. According to that philosophy, the cosmos *is* God, uncreated, existing from eternity; it has no need of a creator, it is all-sufficient, necessary, it is consistency itself. At most, it requires a *demiurge* to put it in order, for order is preceded by chaos. For Aristotle, the stars are gods, 'distinct substances', eternal, outside any 'becoming': astronomy is not a physical science but a theology. Nor can the uncreated stars ever perish. Since a becoming, from birth to death, must be recognized in our sublunary world, it was said to be cyclic, recurring: time chases its own tail. This is the 'endless returning' of the metaphysics, cosmogonies and mythologies of pagan antiquity.

When it affirms that the world was created, the Bible is contradicting all 'star-worship': the stars are not divinities but things that have been created; they are not eternal, but came into being at a given moment; and at a given moment God is able to bring them to an end; the world had a beginning, and it will have an end. All these propositions were scandalously offensive to the Hellenic mind.

God 'has accredited [the man] to all of us, by raising him up from the dead'. The Jewish doctrine of the resurrection of the dead was still more incomprehensible (if that were possible) to a Greek philosopher than the idea of creation. The mystery religions had done something in those days to make the idea of an immortality of the soul familiar: the soul set free from the body to which it had had the misfortune to be bound. But the Judaeo-Christian teaching on the resurrection is quite a different matter.

It does not mean that a part of man—his soul—will be freed by discarding the other part—his material body; biblical teaching implies that the *whole* of man will be saved. It is particularly opposed to the Orphic theory of a fall of souls into evil bodies, to that of the existence of souls anterior to their bodily life, and to metensomatosis, transmigration or re-embodiment of souls. Immortality of the soul is nothing but the soul's *return* to its previous state, its primitive condition before it had fallen into evil matter. The Bible does not regard matter as evil, and the resurrection of men is parallel to the prophetical idea of a renewal of the whole universe: 'See where I create new heavens and a new earth' (Isa. 65: 17).

Just as Greek cosmology, consistently with a metaphysic and a theology, could not receive the idea of the world being created, so Greek anthropology, which also reflected a theology, could not understand or accept the doctrine of the resurrection of man.

There were plenty of other points of incompatibility between ancient pagan thought and that of the Bible; its teaching about time, for instance, which affirms the irreversibility of God's creative deed which tends towards an end, as against the 'eternal returning' of paganism. The same opposition, for the same reasons, between Christianity and the old philosophy has gone on ever since St. Paul stood up on the Areopagus at Athens, from Plotinus to Spinoza.

Socrates
(4th century B.C. *carving*)

Saint Paul
(14th century A.D. *carving*)

Between Athens and Corinth

CONTINUATION OF THE JOURNEY

Paul left Athens after this, and went to Corinth. Here he met a Jew named Aquila, born in Pontus, who, with his wife Priscilla, had lately come from Italy, when Claudius decreed that all Jews should leave Rome. He paid them a visit: then since they were brothers of the same craft (both were tent-makers) he stayed and worked with them. Every sabbath he held a disputation in the synagogue, trying to convince both Jews and Greeks by confronting them with the name of the Lord Jesus. Just at the time when Silas and Timothy arrived from Macedonia, Paul was much occupied with preaching, while he bore witness to the Jews that Jesus was the Christ. . . .

But Crispus, the ruler of the synagogue, learned to believe in the Lord, and so did all his household; and by now many of the Corinthians listened and found faith, and were baptized.

And the Lord said to Paul in a vision at night, 'Do not be afraid, speak out, and refuse to be silenced; I am with thee, and none shall come near to do thee harm; I have a great following in this city.' So he remained there a year and six months, preaching the word of God among them.

Then, when Gallio was proconsul of Achaia, the Jews made a concerted attack on Paul, and dragged him before the judgement-seat. 'This fellow,' they said, 'is persuading men to worship God in a manner the law forbids.' Paul was just opening his mouth to speak, when Gallio said to the Jews, 'It would be only right for me to listen to you Jews with patience, if we had here some wrong done, or some malicious contrivance; but the questions you raise are a matter of words and names, of the law which holds good among yourselves. You must see to it: I have no mind to try such cases.' And he drove them away from the judgement-seat.

Thereupon there was a general onslaught upon Sosthenes, the ruler of the synagogue, who was beaten before the judgement-seat; but all this caused Gallio no concern. (Acts 18: 1–5, 8–17.)

In 146 B.C. Corinth had been burnt down by the consul Memmius, but in 44 B.C. Caesar had made it a colony, peopling it with Italians and orientals; probably the Hellenic part of the population was small, but Greek was still the common language. The city was of considerable commercial importance. An inscription found at Delphi fixes the date of Gallio's proconsulship,

Inscription that enables Paul's stay at Corinth to be dated. Gallio's name is in the fourth line

Corinth

and consequently that of Paul's first stay in Corinth, between
the end of 50 and the end of 52. It was from Corinth that he
wrote the first of his letters that have survived, those to the
Thessalonians: 'Paul and Silvanus and Timothy, to the church
assembled at Thessalonica in God the Father and the Lord
Jesus Christ: grace be yours and peace . . .'.

Paul stayed on many days yet, then took leave of the brethren
and sailed off to Syria; before he left Cenchrae he shaved his
head, since he was under a vow. He took Priscilla and Aquila
with him, but left them behind when he reached Ephesus. He
himself went to the synagogue and reasoned with the Jews, who
asked him to make a longer stay. But he would not consent;
he said, as he took leave of them, 'I will come back to you again,
if it is God's will,' and departed from Ephesus by sea. On
landing at Caesarea, he went up from there to greet the church,
then went down again to Antioch. (Acts 18: 18–22.)

CORINTH: *THE TWO WISDOMS*

The check which St. Paul met from the synagogue confirmed him in his calling to be the apostle of the Gentiles; and his failure with the philosophers at Athens also had its lessons for him.

At Corinth he no longer addressed himself to elders, philosophers, the learned and influential of this world; instead, he turned to a proletariat, indeed, to what Marx called the *Lumpenproletariat*: the dockers, the slaves, the small artisans, all the toilers of a cosmopolitan port. Corinth had the reputation of being a licentious town, it was Aphrodite's city; and it was here, among its proletariat, that he raised a fine Christian community, one of the richest in charisms and spiritual gifts. Christ had sent him to preach the gospel to them, but not with lofty rhetoric, 'lest the cross of Christ might be robbed of its force'.

To those who court their own ruin, the message of the cross is but folly; to us, who are on the way to salvation, it is the evidence of God's power. So we read in scripture, 'I will confound the wisdom of wise men, disappoint the calculations of the prudent.' What has become of the wise men, the scribes, the philosophers of this age we live in? Must we not say that God has turned our worldly wisdom to folly? When God shewed us his wisdom, the world, with all its wisdom, could not find its way to God; and now God would use a foolish thing, our preaching, to save those who will believe in it. Here are the Jews asking for signs and wonders, here are the Greeks intent on their philosophy; but what we preach is Christ crucified; to the Jews, a discouragement, to the Gentiles, mere folly; but to us who have been called, Jew and Gentile alike, Christ the power of God, Christ the wisdom of God. So much wiser than men is God's foolishness; so much stronger than men is God's weakness.

Consider, brethren, the circumstances of your own calling; not many of you are wise, in the world's fashion, not many powerful, not many well-born. No, God has chosen what the world holds foolish, so as to abash the wise, God has chosen what the world holds weak, so as to abash the strong. God has chosen what the world holds base and contemptible, nay, has chosen what is nothing, so as to bring to nothing what is now in being; no human creature was to have any ground for boasting,

'The Greeks intent on their philosophy'
(1 Cor. 1: 22)

(Aphrodite and the seasons)

'What we preach is Christ crucified'
(1 Cor. 1: 23)

(Perpignan)

in the presence of God. It is from him that you take your origin, through Christ Jesus, whom God gave us to be all our wisdom, our justification, our sanctification, and our atonement; so that the scripture might be fulfilled, 'If anyone boasts, let him make his boast in the Lord.'

So it was, brethren, that when I came to you and preached Christ's message to you, I did so without any high pretensions to eloquence, or to philosophy. I had no thought of bringing you any other knowledge than that of Jesus Christ, and of him as crucified. It was with distrust of myself, full of anxious fear, that I approached you; my preaching, my message depended on no persuasive language, devised by human wisdom, but rather on the proof I gave you of spiritual power; God's power, not man's wisdom, was to be the foundation of your faith.

There is, to be sure, a wisdom which we make known among those who are fully grounded; but it is not the wisdom of this world, or of this world's rulers, whose power is to be abrogated. What we make known is the wisdom of God, his secret, kept hidden till now; so, before the ages, God had decreed, reserving glory for us. (None of the rulers of this world could read his secret, or they would not have crucified him to whom all glory belongs.) So we read of, Things no eye has seen, no ear has heard, no human heart conceived, the welcome God has prepared for those who love him.

To us, then, God has made a revelation of it through his Spirit; there is no depth in God's nature so deep that the Spirit cannot find it out. Who else can know a man's thoughts, except the man's own spirit that is within him? So no one else can know God's thoughts, but the Spirit of God. And what we have received is no spirit of worldly wisdom; it is the Spirit that comes from God, to make us understand God's gifts to us; gifts which we make known, not in such words as human wisdom teaches, but in words taught us by the Spirit, matching what is spiritual with what is spiritual. Mere man with his natural gifts cannot take in the thoughts of God's Spirit; they seem mere folly to him, and he cannot grasp them, because they demand a scrutiny which is spiritual. Whereas the man who has spiritual gifts can scrutinize everything, without being subject, himself, to any other man's scrutiny. Who has entered into the mind of the Lord, so as to be able to instruct him? And Christ's mind is ours. (1 Cor. 1: 18 to 2: 16.)

THIRD MISSIONARY JOURNEY
(from 52 or 53 to 57 or 58)

After staying for a time at Antioch, St. Paul traversed Galatia and Phrygia, encouraging the brethren there. Then he returned to Ephesus, as he had promised.

It was while Apollo was away at Corinth that Paul finished his journey through the inland country, and came to Ephesus. He met some disciples there and asked them, 'Was the Holy Spirit given to you, when you learned to believe?' 'Why,' they said, 'nobody even mentioned to us the existence of a Holy Spirit.' 'What baptism, then, did you receive?' Paul asked; and they said, 'John's baptism.' So Paul told them, 'John baptized to bring men to repentance; but he bade the people have faith in one who was to come after him, that is, in Jesus.'

On hearing this, they received baptism in the name of the Lord Jesus; and when Paul laid his hands upon them, the Holy Spirit came down on them, and they spoke with tongues, and prophesied. In all, these men were about twelve in number.

And now he went into the synagogue, and for three months spoke boldly there, reasoning with them and trying to convince them about the kingdom of God; but since there were some who hardened their hearts and refused belief, discrediting the way of the Lord in the eyes of the multitude, he left them, and withdrew his own disciples, holding disputations daily in the school of a certain Tyrannus. This lasted for two years, so that the Lord's word came to the ears of all those who lived in Asia, both Jews and Greeks. (Acts 19: 1–10.)

Many believers came forward, confessing their evil practices and giving a full account of them; and a number of those who followed magic arts made their books into a heap and burned them in public . . . (Acts 19: 18–19.)

When all this was over, the thought in Paul's heart was to go to Jerusalem, first travelling through Macedonia and Achaia; 'When I have been there,' he said, 'I must go on and see Rome.' And he sent on two of those who ministered to him, Timothy and Erastus, into Macedonia, but waited for a while himself in Asia. It was just at this time that the way of the Lord was the cause of a notable disturbance. (Acts 19: 21–23.)

The stir was caused by a silversmith named Demetrius, who made votive models of the shrine of the goddess Artemis (Diana). Paul's preaching was damaging this man's trade, and he called a meeting of his fellow craftsmen, to whom he pointed out the harm being done both to their business and to the repute of the goddess. With cries of 'Great is Artemis of the Ephesians!' they proceeded to stir up the

The Ephesian Artemis

people, and a serious riot ensued, which was eventually quelled by the tact of the town-clerk. 'When the tumult was over, Paul summoned his disciples, to rally their spirits and bid them farewell, and set out on his journey into Macedonia. He passed through all that region, and gave them much encouragement; then he entered Greece' (Acts 20: 1–2). and stayed there three months.

In his *St. Paul's Journies*, Henri Metzger writes: 'The book of Acts tells us nothing about the reasons that sent St. Paul on this journey into Macedonia and Achaia, and he is himself sparing of details; still, there are passages in the Epistles which do something to satisfy our curiosity. We learn that the main object of the projected trip to Jerusalem was to take the yield of the collections for relief made among the communities he had founded. On the other hand, in 1 Corinthians 16: 2 ff. there is a clear allusion to a stay of the apostle at Corinth, which cannot be the long ministry of the years 50–51, nor yet the journey proposed in Acts 20: 1–3.'

Paul writes at the end of his first letter to the Corinthians: 'And now about the collection which is being made for the saints; follow the plan which I have prescribed for the Galatian churches. Each of you should put aside, on the first day of the week, what he can afford to spare, and save it up, so that there may be no need for a collection at the time of my visit ... I shall be coming to you as soon as I have made the round of Macedonia (I mean to go round Macedonia), and perhaps stay with you or even pass the winter with you ... This is no occasion for a mere passing visit to you; I hope to spend some time with you, if the Lord will let me. Till Pentecost, I shall be staying at Ephesus; a great opportunity lies open to me, plain to view, and strong forces oppose me' (1 Cor. 16: 1–9).

'The short visit that St. Paul made to the Corinthians will have been about the middle or end of the year 55, simply a trip to and fro from Ephesus, which was the headquarters of his activities during these crucial years. We learn in the second letter to the Corinthians about the beginning of the last journey to Macedonia. As on the first occasion, St. Paul embarked at Troas, no doubt after having stayed there for a time and preached the Gospel. No indication of his route is given this time and, when he got to Macedonia, he met nothing but difficulties—"all was conflict without, all was anxiety within" (2 Cor. 7: 5). He then went on to Corinth (the Acts only specifies Greece, saying he was there for three months)' (Metzger, *op. cit.*, pp. 45–46). It was during this time at Corinth that Paul wrote the Epistle to the Romans.

'. . . he was meaning to take ship for Syria; but, finding that the Jews were plotting against him, he resolved to go back again through Macedonia' (Acts 20: 3). Metzger points out that no details are given of the third visit to Macedonia, except that certain delegates preceded Paul to Troas, while he and those of his companions who reported these things ('we') spent Easter at Philippi, and rejoined the others 'as soon as the time of unleavened bread was over'.

It is to be noticed that the narrative in the Acts continues in the first person from this point, and again supplies a number of facts. 'As soon as the time of unleavened bread was over, we set sail from Philippi, and took five days to reach them at Troas, where we spent seven days' (Acts 20: 6). It was here and now that a young man called Eutychus had a fatal accident, and was raised to life by Paul. 'For ourselves, we took ship and sailed to Assos, where we were to take Paul on board; he had arranged this, because he himself meant to go across by land. So at Assos we met him, and took him on board, and journeyed to Mitylene. Sailing thence, we reached a point opposite Chios the following day; on the next, we put in at Samos, and arrived on the third at Miletus. Paul had made up his mind to sail past Ephesus, for fear of having to waste time in Asia; he was eager, if he found it possible, to keep the day of Pentecost at Jerusalem' (Acts 20: 13–16). From Miletus he sent for the elders of the church at Ephesus, and when they were come he said to them:

'Now, a prisoner in spirit, I am going up to Jerusalem, knowing nothing of what is to befall me there; only, as I go on from city to city, the Holy Spirit assures me that at Jerusalem, bondage and affliction await me. . . . Here, then, I stand, well

144

knowing that you will not see my face again; you, among whom I came and went, preaching the kingdom of God. . . .

'Keep watch, then, over yourselves, and over God's Church, in which the Holy Spirit has made you bishops; you are to be the shepherds of that flock which he won for himself at the price of his own blood. I know well that ravening wolves will come among you when I am gone, and will not spare the flock; there will be men among your own number who will come forward with a false message, and find disciples to follow them. . . .'

When he had said this, he knelt down and prayed with them all. They all wept abundantly, and embraced Paul and kissed him, grieving most over what he had said about never seeing his face again. And so they escorted him to the ship.

When we tore ourselves away from them, and at last put out to sea, we made a straight course, sailing to Cos, and next day to Rhodes, and thence to Patara. There, finding a ship crossing to Phoenice, we went on board and set sail. We sighted Cyprus, but passed it on our left, and held on for Syria, where we landed at Tyre . . . Here we enquired for the brethren, and made a stay of seven days with them; they, by revelation, warned Paul not to go up to Jerusalem. . . .

The end of our voyage brought us from Tyre to Ptolemais, where we greeted the brethren and stayed one day with them; the day after, we left them and arrived at Caesarea. . . . When the time came to an end, we made all ready, and went up to Jerusalem. (Acts 20: 22–30, 36–38; 21: 1–8, 15.)

PAUL'S GOSPEL: BEING-IN-CHRIST

The gospel that St. Paul preached is the great tidings that by baptism and faith we are grafted into Christ; and that we thus share in the oil—the Spirit—of the olive tree which is Israel, the people of God, through him who is the Anointed of God.

If there is one expression that is characteristic of Paul's language and thought, which bears his mark and is constantly repeated, it is 'in Christ', 'in Christ Jesus', 'in Him'. He is our root, the stock from which we grow: 'Go on, then, ordering your lives in Christ Jesus our Lord, according to the tradition you have received of him. You are to be rooted in him, built up on him . . .'

'We who were taken up into Christ by baptism have been taken up, all of us, into his death' (Rom. 6: 3).
(13th century psalter of Besancon)

(Col. 2: 6–7). He is the foundation on which we are based and built: 'With what grace God has bestowed on me, I have laid a foundation as a careful architect should; it is left for someone else to build upon it. Only, whoever builds on it must be careful how he builds. The foundation which has been laid is the only one which anybody can lay; I mean Jesus Christ' (1 Cor. 3: 10–11). And not only the foundation but the corner-stone too, which shapes and holds the building together: 'Apostles and prophets are the foundation on which you were built, and the chief corner-stone of it is Jesus Christ himself. In him the whole fabric is bound together, as it grows into a temple, dedicated to the Lord; in him you too are being built in with the rest, so that God may find in you a dwelling-place for his Spirit' (Eph. 2: 20-22). The letters to the Thessalonians begin: 'Paul . . . to the church assembled at Thessalonica *in* God the Father and the Lord Jesus Christ'.

BEING-WITH-CHRIST

The only characteristically Pauline words that equal 'in Christ' in frequency are those expressing the idea of 'being-with-Christ'.

You know well enough that we who were taken up into Christ by baptism have been taken up, all of us, into his death. In our baptism, we have been buried with him, died like him, that so, just as Christ was raised up by his Father's power from the dead, we too might live and move in a new kind of existence. We have to be closely fitted into the pattern of his resurrection, as we have been into the pattern of his death; we have to be sure of this, that our former nature has been crucified with him. . . . And if we have died with Christ, we have faith to believe that we shall also share his life. We know that Christ, now he has risen from the dead, cannot die any more; death has no more power over him (Rom. 6: 3–9). And if we are his children, then we are his heirs too; heirs of God, sharing the inheritance of Christ; only we must share his sufferings, if we are to share his glory (Rom. 8: 17). With Christ I hang upon the cross, and yet I am alive; or rather, not I; it is Christ that lives in me (Gal. 2: 20). You, by baptism, have been united with his burial, united, too, with his resurrection, through your faith in that exercise of power by which God raised him from the dead (Col. 2: 12). How rich God is in mercy, with what an excess of love he loved us! Our sins had made dead men of us, and he, in giving life to Christ, gave life to us too; it is his grace that has saved you; raised us up too, enthroned us too above the heavens, in Christ Jesus (Eph. 2: 4–6).

Risen, then, with Christ, you must lift your thoughts above, where Christ now sits at the right hand of God (Col. 3: 1). We are to share his life, because we have shared his death; if we endure, we shall reign with him (2 Tim. 2: 11–12). In giving life to him, he gave life to you too, when you lay dead in your sins (Col. 2: 13). . . . what it means to share his sufferings, moulded into the pattern of his death, in the hope of achieving resurrection from the dead (Phil. 3: 10). All those who from the first were known to him, he has destined from the first to be moulded into the image of his Son (Rom. 8: 29). He will form this humbled body of ours anew, moulding it into the image of his glorified body (Phil. 3: 21). The Gentiles are to win the *same* inheritance, to be made part of the *same* body, to share the *same* divine promise, in Christ Jesus (Eph. 3: 6). In him you too are being built in with the rest, so that God may find in you a dwelling-place for his Spirit (Eph. 2: 22).

THE CHURCH THE BODY OF CHRIST

This fellowship with Christ in his life, in his death, his resurrection and his divine life, is no metaphor: it is a reality. We are grafted into him, and through him we share in the life of the Body which is his people, the Church.

This fellowship and participation in Christ's life is not simply a 'private' and individual fellowship with God, as Plotinus would have it. It is a matter of a whole people which is grafted into, built up upon, Christ, and each member of this people is in fellowship with each and all of the others who share in that Life. 'Just so we, though many in number, form one body in Christ, and each acts as the counterpart of another' (Rom. 12: 5).

And this unity of the Body that we form is not a metaphor either: it is an ontological reality, though neither physical nor visible. Christ is 'the head to which the whole Church is joined, so that the Church is his body . . . ; membership of the body binds us to one another . . . ; we are limbs of his body' (Eph. 1: 22, 4: 25, 5: 30). Already in the books of the Jewish prophets, God's people is looked on as a unity, a *person*, whom the Lord speaks to as to his loved one; 'With unchanging love I love thee . . . Israel, poor homeless maid' (Jer. 31: 2). The word church, *ekklesia*, meaning an 'assembly called together', a 'congregation', translates the Hebrew *qahal*. The Church is the *qahal* of the new Israel.

The Bible is the love story of God and the beloved with whom he has established a bridal relationship (cf. Ezekiel 16). It is the agelong tradition of Jewish mysticism, as of Christian mysticism, that the book called the Song of Songs is the key to all the Scriptures, for it enshrines the secret of secrets—God's bridal love for his bride. 'Your name,' says the maiden of the Song to

148

her beloved, 'your name is as oil that is poured out'. And that name is Messiah, he who has been anointed with the oil of gladness, the efficacious sign of the Spirit of God.

St. Paul makes this tradition his own in the famous passage of Ephesians which is read in the marriage Mass of the Roman rite:

> You who are husbands must shew love to your wives, as Christ shewed love to the Church when he gave himself up on its behalf. He would hallow it, purify it by bathing it in the water to which his word gave life; he would summon it into his own presence, the Church in all its beauty, no stain, no wrinkle, no such disfigurement; it was to be holy, it was to be spotless. And that is how husband ought to love wife, as if she were his own body; in loving his wife, a man is but loving himself. It is unheard of, that a man should bear ill-will to his own flesh and blood; no, he keeps it fed and warmed; and so it is with Christ and his Church; we are limbs of his body; flesh and bone, we belong to him. That is why a man will leave his father and mother and will cling to his wife, and the two will become one flesh. Yes, those words are a high mystery, and I am applying them here to Christ and his Church. (Eph. 5: 25–32.)

In the gospels, fullness, fulfilment, is likened to a wedding-feast —'the wedding-feast of the Lamb', says the Apocalypse of St. John.

*Christ, Bridegroom
of the Church
(14th century)*

This Body of Christ is the Temple of the Holy Spirit. St. Paul makes use of the images both of body and of building to signify this organic reality founded on Christ, the Church. 'Do you not understand that you are God's temple, and that God's Spirit has his dwelling in you?' (1 Cor. 3: 16).

The Lord was already to be found dwelling in Israel. Jehovah made his habitation among his people, living with and in them. 'And you are the temple of the living God; God has told us so; I will live and move among them, and be their God, and they shall be my people' (2 Cor. 6: 16; cf. Lev. 26: 12). The Temple of the living God that we are, built of living stones (cf. 1 Peter 2: 5), is the temple that the prophets promised to David and Solomon: 'This too the Lord promises, that he will grant thy line continuance. So, when thy days are ended, and thou art laid to rest beside thy fathers, I will grant thee for successor a son of thy own body, established firmly on his throne. He it is that shall build a house to do my name honour. I will prolong for ever his royal dynasty' (2 Sam. 7: 11–13).

St. Paul mingles the images of body and building in a way that sometimes borders on the fantastic: 'Apostles and prophets are the foundation on which you were built, and the chief corner-stone of it is Jesus Christ himself. In him the whole fabric is bound together, as it *grows* into a temple, dedicated to the Lord; in whom you too are being built in with the rest, so that God may find in you a dwelling-place for his Spirit' (Eph. 2: 20–22). 'Some he has appointed to be apostles, others to be prophets, others to be evangelists, or pastors, or teachers. They are to . . . build up the frame of Christ's body . . . We are to . . . *grow up*, in everything, into a due proportion with Christ, who is our head. On him all the body depends; it is organized and unified by each contact with the source which supplies it . . .' (Eph. 4: 11–16).

Christ is 'that head of ours, on whom all the body depends, supplied and unified by joint and ligament; and so growing up with a growth which is divine' (Col. 2: 19).

THE INDWELLING OF THE HOLY SPIRIT

St. Paul consistently teaches that the Holy Spirit dwells in us. For example, in Romans 8: 9, 'You live the life of the spirit, not the life of nature; that is, if the Spirit of God dwells in you'; and two verses later: 'If the spirit of him who raised up Jesus from the dead dwells in you, he who raised up Jesus Christ from the dead will give life to your perishable bodies too, for the sake of his Spirit who dwells in you.'

The Spirit within us is an earnest of the promise that we are to be the children of God; and as well as the earnest, the active leaven which will transform us, from being 'psychic' man, into a new being, a spiritual body, a child of God. By this anointing of the Spirit we become like Christ: 'It is God who gives both us and you our certainty in Christ; it is he who has anointed (*khrisas*) us, just as it is he who has put his seal on us, and given us the foretaste of his Spirit in our hearts' (2 Cor. 1: 21–22). It is through the Spirit that we perceive that we are called to adoption: 'The Spirit himself thus assures our spirit, that we are children of God . . . As before, the Spirit comes to the aid of our

weakness; when we do not
know what prayer to offer,
to pray as we ought, the
Spirit himself intercedes
for us, with groans beyond
all utterance' (Rom. 8: 16,
26).

Faith, the knowledge of
God, would be impossible
for us were it not for this
indwelling of his Spirit:
'There is no depth in
God's nature so deep that
the Spirit cannot find it out. Who else can know a man's
thoughts, except the man's own spirit that is within him? So no
one else can know God's thoughts, but the Spirit of God. And
what we have received is no spirit of worldly wisdom; it is the
Spirit that comes from God, to make us understand God's gifts
to us' (1 Cor. 2: 10–12). In the next section we shall see that
it is also through the Holy Spirit that God's *agape* becomes
possible in us.

God's presence in his people, his Church, is active, working,
creative and transforming. That people is a body, and God works
in it with the free and conscious co-operation of the cells, the
persons, who compose that body. Here we come to what must
be called St. Paul's philosophy of action. 'On their arrival, they
called the Church together, and told the story of all God *had done
to aid them*, and how, through faith, he had left a door open for
the Gentiles' (Acts 14: 26). 'When they reached Jerusalem,
they were welcomed by the church, and by the apostles and
presbyters; and they told them of all that God *had done to aid
them*' (Acts 15: 4). 'Then the whole company kept silence, and
listened to Barnabas and Paul describing all the signs and
wonders God had performed among the Gentiles *by their means*'
(Acts 15: 12). Paul writes to the quarrelling Corinthians:

> When one of you says, 'I am for Paul,' and another, 'I am
> for Apollo,' are not these human thoughts? Why, what is

Apollo, what is Paul? Only the ministers of the God in whom your faith rests, who have brought that faith to each of you in the measure God granted. It was for me to plant the seed, for Apollo to water it, but it was God who gave the increase. And if so, the man who plants, the man who waters, count for nothing; God is everything, since it is he who gives the increase. This man plants, that man waters; it is all one. And yet either will receive his own wages, in proportion to his own work. . . . we are only his assistants. (1 Cor. 3: 4–9.)

There are different kinds of gifts, though it is the same Spirit who gives them, just as there are different kinds of service, though it is the same Lord we serve, and different manifestations of power, though it is the same God who manifests his power everywhere in all of us. The revelation of the Spirit is imparted to each, to make the best advantage of it. One learns to speak with wisdom, by the power of the Spirit, another to speak with knowledge, with the same Spirit for his rule; one, through the same Spirit, is given faith; another, through the same Spirit, powers of healing; one can perform miracles, one can prophesy, another can test the spirit of the prophets; one can speak in different tongues, another can interpret the tongues; but all this is the work of one and the same Spirit, who distributes his gifts to each as he will severally.

A man's body is all one, though it has a number of different organs; and all this multitude of organs goes to make up one body; so it is with Christ. We too, all of us, have been baptized into a single body by the power of a single Spirit, Jews and Greeks, slaves and free men alike; we have all been given drink at a single source, the one Spirit. The body, after all, consists not of one organ, but of many. (1 Cor. 12: 4–14.)

Man's activity is grafted into and grows from God's; God's activity is at work in man's. 'In him we live, and move, and have our being'. God's activity makes use of ours, but at the same time respects it; his freedom acts within ours. 'Both the will to do it and the accomplishment of that will are something which God accomplishes in you, to carry out his living purpose' (Phil. 2: 13); 'He whose power is at work in us' (Eph. 3: 20); 'I strive so anxiously; and with effect, so effectually does his power manifest itself in me' (Col. 1: 29); 'God's message, not man's; it is

God, after all, who manifests his power in you that have learned to believe' (1 Thess. 2: 13).

God's doing at work in our doing takes nothing at all from our freedom. On the contrary, it livens, cleanses and strengthens it: 'Where the Lord's Spirit is, there is freedom' (2 Cor. 3: 17). Our freedom is not fulfilled in solitary withdrawal and ignoring of God, but in co-operation with him for his work and glory. Freedom does not consist in being able to choose to say Yes or No to God: freedom is Yes. To choose sin is to be enslaved. If we are set free by the Spirit of the Son, then we are really free, and are also sons. We fulfil and show forth our freedom by making it fruitful, not by shutting ourselves up in the loneliness of negation.

The flowering of created liberty in face of the liberty of God is certainly a mystery; it is the mystery of mysteries, the mystery of the Creation. Descartes wrote: 'The Lord has done three wonders: something out of nothing, free will, and the God-man.'

AGAPE

The bond that secures the life and organic unity of this spiritual Body is *agape*.

In Latin this word is rendered *caritas*, and in English 'charity', or sometimes 'love', but we have no word that translates the *agape* of the Bible exactly: neither love nor charity is its equivalent. The word 'love' has all the associations that romance and 'nature mysticisms'—the mystery religions of modern times—have given to it. From *Tristram and Iseult* to the romanticism of the nineteenth and twentieth centuries, the *mystique* of love as *eros* has been a religion, wherein *eros* is associated with hopelessness and a desire for death: 'I am going to tell you a tale of love and death . . .' Christian *agape* is just the opposite: it is not idolatrous, an exercise in worshipping what is created; it does not lead to empty negation—it is life and hope. There are no love-potions in *agape*, no enslavement, no enchantments, no despair; it is not a love that destroys, it creates; it does not bring sorrow, but happiness and peace. If we look for an illustration

'Agape, misce nobis'
(Catacombs, 4th century)

in music, we may think of love that bewitches in Wagner and of Christian love in Bach.

Neither can *agape* be properly translated charity, nowadays. Etymologically charity indeed comes from *caritas*, but it has lost its original meaning. The word has been devalued, in consequence of an inflation of the language of sacred things, indicative of a fall in spiritual intensity. Like the manna in the hands of the disobedient Hebrews, sacred words have decomposed, 'gone rotten'; there is no longer any gold behind the money of language. Where the Spirit has gone out of us, there we are left only with words in decay; they stink, as Martha said of the dead body of her brother Lazarus. There is the same corruption of language as of sacred art, and for the same reason.

Agape is a specifically biblical and Christian idea. The word itself is hardly to be found in either classical or current Greek; the New Testament writers took it from the Septuagint, where it translates the Hebrew *ahaba*. We have to fall back on the word charity, strictly in the original sense, which is now technical in theology; we use 'love' only when there is no possibility of misunderstanding.

Agape is a supernatural love, coming from God; spiritual, being conferred by the Holy Spirit who dwells in us; free, as all that is of the Spirit is free. It binds together the Lord's followers, 'the saints', making of them one body, the Body of Christ,

155

quickened by his *agape*, sharing in the life of the Blessed Trinity, whose inwardness also is defined essentially by *agape*.

Agape is the very life of the Blessed Trinity. It is the bond between the Father, the Son and the Spirit: 'the Son of his *agape*', 'his beloved Son' (Col. 1: 13). The Spirit is *agape*: 'I entreat you, brethren, by our Lord Jesus Christ, and by the *agape* of the Holy Spirit . . .' (Rom. 15: 30).

Agape is in the first place the love that constitutes the innermost life of God. Then it is the love that he bears towards us.

> But here, as if God meant to prove how well he loves us, it was while we were still sinners that Christ . . . died for us. (Rom. 5: 8.)
>
> Who will come forward to accuse God's elect, when God acquits us? Who will pass sentence against us, when Jesus Christ, who died, nay, has risen again, and sits at the right hand of God, is pleading for us? Who will separate us from the love of Christ? Will affliction, or distress, or persecution, or hunger, or nakedness, or peril, or the sword? For thy sake, says the scripture, we face death at every moment, reckoned no better than sheep marked down for slaughter. Yet in all this we are conquerors, through him who has granted us his love. Of this I am fully persuaded; neither death nor life, no angels or principalities or powers, neither what is present nor what is to come, no force whatever, neither the height above us nor the depth beneath us, nor any other created thing, will be able to separate us from the love of God, which comes to us in Christ Jesus our Lord. (Rom. 8: 33–39.)

It is *in agape* that God, before ever the world was created, predestined us to be adopted as his sons through Jesus Christ, with whom we are heirs (Cf. Eph. 1: 4–5).

Lastly, *agape* is man's love for God, by the Spirit and in Christ, and man's love for man, in the Church which is Christ's Body.

Agape is in essence supernatural and spiritual, for it comes from the Holy Spirit; the *agape* of God 'has been poured out in our hearts by the Holy Spirit, whom we have received' (Rom. 5: 5); 'the spirit yields a harvest of love' (Gal. 5: 22). Our love for our brethren is Christ's love that is in us, 'the love of Christ . . . passes knowledge' (Eph. 3: 19). Paul writes to the Corinthians (2, 5: 14) that 'Christ's love is a compelling motive'.

Christian *agape* is supernatural in the sense that it is a participation in God's life through the Spirit abiding in us and the presence of Christ in his ecclesial Body. *Agape* therefore does not belong to the human order, that biological and psychological order which St. Paul calls the order of 'flesh'. It is not a matter for the psychological analysis of emotional motives. It is the present possession of the earnest of the world to come.

'Charity (*agape*) is the bond (*syndesmos*) which makes us perfect' (Col. 3: 14), and it ensures unity in the growth of the Body, the Church; it builds up (Cf. Eph. 4: 16).

St. Paul attached great importance to knowledge. We have seen that knowledge of the mystery revealed in Christ is the substance of what he preached. For him, faith is not opposed to knowledge, as it was for the gnostics. Faith *is* knowledge, knowledge of God, understanding of the divine mystery shown forth in his Son; and the whole of this book has been devoted to a summary examination of what this divine mystery is that was given to the world.

But Paul knew that spiritual knowledge is nothing without *agape*, without the love of God energizing in us to bring forth fruit. Without *agape*, knowledge of God's mystery would degenerate into a detestable academicism, an academicism of sacred things; instead of a gathering of saints we should have a synagogue of scribes. The Corinthians were very proud of their spiritual learning, and Paul wrote to them: 'Knowledge only breeds self-conceit, it is charity that binds the building together. If anybody claims to have superior knowledge, it means that he has not yet attained the knowledge which is true knowledge; it is only when a man loves God that God acknowledges him' (1 Cor. 8: 1-3). The man who seeks to know *some thing* has not understood about the mystery of God, which is *some one*. This means that all relation of knowing between God and man can only be a relation of loving. Without *agape*, knowledge becomes falsehood, the disciple's betrayal by a treacherous kiss.

I may speak with every tongue that men and angels use; yet, if I lack charity, I am no better than echoing bronze, or the clash of cymbals. I may have powers of prophecy, no secret hidden from me, no knowledge too deep for me; I may have utter faith, so that I can move mountains; yet if I lack charity, I count for nothing. I may give away all that I have, to feed the poor; I may give myself up to be burnt at the stake; if I lack charity, it goes for nothing.

Charity is patient, is kind; charity feels no envy; charity is never perverse or proud, never insolent; does not claim its rights, cannot be provoked, does not brood over an injury; takes no pleasure in wrong-doing but rejoices at the victory of truth; sustains, believes, hopes, endures, to the last.

The time will come when we shall outgrow prophecy, when speaking with tongues will come to an end, when knowledge will be swept away; we shall never have finished with charity. Our knowledge, our prophecy, are only glimpses of the truth; and these glimpses will be swept away when the time of fulfilment comes. (Just so, when I was a child, I talked like a child, I had the intelligence, the thoughts of a child; since I became a man, I have outgrown childish ways.)

At present, we are looking at a confused reflection in a mirror; then, we shall see face to face; now, I have only glimpses of knowledge; then, I shall recognize God as he has recognized me.

Meanwhile, faith, hope and charity persist, all three; but the greatest of them all is charity. (1 Cor. 13.)

There is, then, a 'justification' by charity, as there is a justification by faith. 'Works' are not enough to constitute justness before the sight of God, who is holiness itself. 'Faith that finds

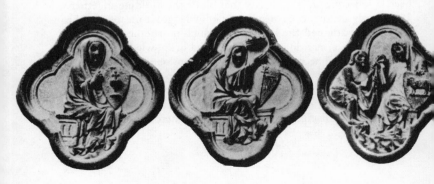

its expression in love' (Gal. 5: 6) is, with hope, the very essence of holiness.

Let us remember once again that, contrary to the Kantian view, charity is so essential to the worth of a moral action that to give all one's property to the poor, or even to sacrifice oneself altogether, is morally worthless if charity does not imbue what we do. This is exactly the opposite of Kant's notion, according to which love spoils the purity of ethical conduct.

The depth-psychology of our day sees clearly how much false virtue and pseudo-morality lurks behind some examples of 'self-sacrificing' behaviour; they are in fact only morbid satisfactions of masochism or of an urge to hurt oneself—'satisfaction of the flesh again', St. Paul would have said. Whatever is without charity abides in death.

WORK

St. Paul earned his living by making tents.

> You will bear me out, that these hands of mine have sufficed for all that I and my companions needed. (Acts 20: 34.)

> Brethren, you can remember how we toiled and laboured, all the time we were preaching God's gospel to you, working day and night so as not to burden you with expense. (1 Thess. 2: 9.)

> You do not need to be reminded how, on our visit, we set you an example to be imitated; we were no vagabonds ourselves. We would not even be indebted to you for our daily bread, we earned it in weariness and toil, working with our hands, night and day, so as not to be a burden to any of you; not that we are obliged to do so, but as a model for your own behaviour; you were to follow our example. The charge we gave you on our visit was that the man who refuses to work must be left to starve. (2 Thess. 3: 7–10.)

> Still, as I write, we go hungry and thirsty and naked; we are mishandled, we have no home to settle in, we are hard put to it, working with our own hands. . . . (1 Cor. 4: 11–12; cf. ch. 9 and 2 Cor. 11: 7–12; 12: 13.)

The fact that St. Paul supported himself deserves thinking about. We have to learn not only from the words of the Lord

'Meanwhile faith, hope and charity persist, all three:
but the greatest of them all is charity'
(1 Cor 13: 13). (Amiens)

159

and of his prophets and apostles, but also from their deeds and their way of life.

In pagan antiquity, working with the hands was looked on as degrading; it was a job for slaves and for those who were considered inferior people; in the *Republic*, Plato assigns work to that category of men whom he regarded as the lowest of the low. The wise man, 'the sage', is the man of leisure, who has slaves and need do no work himself. Here the Marxist *critique* is to the point: a view of the world that opposes the 'sensible' to the 'intelligible' is a result of a social and economic situation in which a working class is exploited by a privileged minority.

This contempt for work, associated with contempt for what is bodily, material, 'sensible', continued to live on in the Manichean and Catharist tradition. Among the Catharists, men were divided into two classes: there were the 'imperfect', who did the work and were married; and there were the 'pure' (*katharoi*) who, neither working nor marrying, were supported by the imperfect, and were thus left free for contemplation. It is still possible to meet among Christian people those who retain something of this mentality.

The whole biblical and evangelical tradition is dead against such an attitude. For the Jews there was no incompatibility between manual work, on the land or of any other kind, and the highest contemplative and mystical life. Paul the tent-maker is the king of Christian thinkers.

CELIBACY AND ASCETICISM

Paul did not marry; during all his missionary life he was alone. He writes to the Corinthians (1, 9: 1–6): 'Am I not free to do as I will? Am I not an apostle, have I not seen our Lord Jesus Christ? Are not you yourselves my achievement in the Lord? . . . Have we not a right to be provided with food and drink; nay, have we not the right to travel about with a woman who is a sister, as the other apostles do, as the Lord's brethren do, and Cephas? Must I and Barnabas, alone among them, be forbidden to do as much?' He says in the same letter (7: 1): 'A man does well to abstain from all commerce with women'; and he writes to the Romans (14: 21): 'Thou doest well if thou refusest to eat meat, or to drink wine . . .'. And to the Corinthians he adds: 'I wish you were all in the same state as myself; but each of us has his own endowment from God, one to live in this way, another in that.'

About virgins, I have no command from the Lord; but I give you my opinion, as one who is, under the Lord's mercy, a true counsellor.

This, then, I hold to be the best counsel in such times of stress, that this is the best condition for man to be in. Art thou yoked to a wife? Then do not go about to free thyself. Art thou free of wedlock? Then do not go about to find a wife. Not that thou dost commit sin if thou marriest; nor, if she marries, has the virgin committed sin. It is only that those who do so will meet with outward distress. But I leave you your freedom.

Only, brethren, I would say this; the time is drawing to an end; nothing remains, but for those who have wives to behave as though they had none; those who weep must forget their tears, and those who rejoice their rejoicing, and those who buy must renounce possession; and those who take advantage of what the world offers must not take full advantage of it; the fashion of this world is soon to pass away.

And I would have you free from concern. He who is un-married is concerned with God's claim, asking how he is to please God; whereas the married man is concerned with the world's claim, asking how he is to please his wife; and thus he is at issue with himself. (1 Cor. 7: 25–33.)

Asceticism has a prophetical significance. It foreshadows, in the very life of the holy person, the human state in the world that is to come, when men shall be as God's angels, neither marrying nor being given in marriage. Christian ascesis antici-pates the future life, and in a measure actualizes it in this world.

Attachment to the conditions of human life as they now are is not in itself wrong, but it is anachronic, 'outdated', for 'the fashion of this world is soon to pass away'. The man who is the integral realist is the ascetic. To be wholly given up to present time is a contradiction. Paul's dialectic of the old and the new man, of man renewed by the life of the Holy Spirit, comes in again here. The spiritual man is even now caught up in the economy of a new and everlasting existence, that of men who are born anew in Christ. Against the Pauline background of the history of creation, asceticism takes on meaning. This world, this world's time, are already out of date. Christian asceticism emphasizes this outwornness of present time and bears witness to the presence within it of the time that is to come: asceticism is turned towards the Lord's coming again. The old man, 'carnal man', does not understand this standpoint, this new thing in God's work. The spiritual man is essentially the prophetical man who can discern the coming of the new world here and now: 'What we can see, lasts but for a moment; what is unseen is eternal' (2 Cor. 4: 18).

The excellence of celibacy, because of the freedom it allows, does not at all imply any Manicheism in regard to marriage in Paul's thought. In the Pastoral Epistles he speaks out prophetically against Catharism in all its forms: 'We are expressly told by inspiration that, in later days, there will be some who abandon the faith, listening to false inspirations, and doctrines taught by the devils. They will be deceived by the pretensions of impostors, whose conscience is hardened as if by a searing-iron. Such teachers bid them abstain from marriage, and from certain kinds of food, although God has made these for the grateful enjoyment of those whom faith has enabled to recognize the truth. All is good that God has made, nothing is to be rejected; only we must be thankful to him when we partake of it, then it is hallowed for our use by God's blessing and the prayer which brings it' (1 Tim. 4: 1–5); 'As if anything could be unclean for those who have clean hearts! But for these men, defiled as they are by want of faith, everything is unclean; defilement has entered their very thought, their very consciences' (Titus 1: 15). There is nothing more foreign to biblical tradition than a Manichean attitude towards the things of sense, towards the life of the body and its fruitfulness. The world in its wholeness is mystery, and that Paul appreciated the mystery of marriage is shown by his words to the Ephesians, already quoted: 'those words are a high mystery . . .'.

But precisely because the world is mystery it is good that some should abstain from using the world, in order that it may be known as the prophetical mystery that it is. It is good to use the world as if not using it, for the world as we see it is passing away, giving place to the world to come which it foreshadows. So bachelors and maidens as well as married people show forth the mystery of marriage. Marriage ceases to be experienced as a mystery if there be no chosen celibacy to mark its eschatological meaning, and the mystery ceases to be consecrated in its 'sensible' forms if man knows not woman.

For the rest, nobody is more human than Paul the ascetic, who writes solicitously to Timothy (1, 5: 23), 'Do not confine thyself to water any longer; take a little wine to relieve thy stomach, and thy frequent attacks of illness.'

Paul was a fighter, and fighting images recur constantly in his letters. They show beyond question that he was full of the spirit of attack, transfigured and made fertile by holiness. He was an athlete of Christ. 'You know well enough that when men run in a race, the race is for all, but the prize for one; run, then, for victory. Every athlete must keep all his appetites under control; and he does it to win a crown that fades, whereas ours is imperishable. So I do not run my course like a man in doubt of his goal: I do not fight my battle like a man who wastes his blows on the air. I buffet my own body, and make it my slave; or I, who have preached to others, may myself be rejected as worthless' (1 Cor. 9: 24–27). Paul's asceticism is the training of an athlete: there is nothing morbid about it, no barren self-affliction; it is directed essentially towards the obtaining of results —a tree is pruned in order that it may bear more fruit.

St. Paul was no seeker after the past, given to 'la recherche du temps perdu'. Writing to the Philippians, he says that he does not claim to have won the prize of perfection, but he presses on, in the hope that he may attain it: and 'this at least I do; forgetting what I have left behind, intent on what lies before me,

I press on with the goal in view, eager for the prize, God's
heavenly summons in Christ Jesus' (Phil. 3: 13–14).

WEAKNESS-STRENGTH

Was St. Paul a sick man? Plenty of theories have been enun-
ciated about this, as has already been said. What is certain is
that he speaks of a weakness, an infirmity of the flesh, that he
cannot get rid of. He reminds the Galatians (4: 13–15) that it
was owing to sickness that he first preached to them and that
they had borne patiently with his trial, which was theirs also:
receiving him 'as God's angel, as Christ Jesus . . . I assure you,
you would have plucked out your eyes, if you had the chance,
and given them to me'. And to the Corinthians he recalls that
he came to them in weakness and fear and much trembling (cf.
I, 2: 3).

Referring to Paul, the Lord had said to Ananias that 'I have
yet to tell him, how much suffering he will have to undergo for
my name's sake' (Acts 9: 16). And Paul tells the Corinthians
what in fact his life as an apostle was like.

Christ's humiliation
prefigured by Job and Lamech
(Biblia Pauperum, 15th century)

It seems as if God had destined us, his apostles, to be in the lowest place of all, like men under sentence of death; such a spectacle do we present to the whole creation, men and angels alike. We are fools for Christ's sake, you are so wise; we are so helpless, you so stout of heart; you are held in honour, while we are despised. Still, as I write, we go hungry and thirsty and naked; we are mishandled, we have no home to settle in, we are hard put to it, working with our own hands. Men revile us, and we answer with a blessing, persecute us, and we make the best of it, speak ill of us, and we fall to entreaty. We are still the world's refuse; everybody thinks himself well rid of us. (1 Cor. 4: 9–13.)

Again, speaking of false apostles in his second letter to the same, he relates what he has to put up with.

Are they Hebrews? So am I. Are they Israelites? So am I. Are they descended from Abraham? So am I. Are they Christ's servants? These are wild words; I am something more. I have toiled harder, spent longer days in prison, been beaten so cruelly, so often looked death in the face. Five times the Jews scourged me, and spared me but one lash in the forty; three times I was beaten with rods, once I was stoned; I have been shipwrecked three times, I have spent a night and a day as a castaway at sea. What journeys I have undertaken, in danger from rivers, in danger from robbers, in danger from my own people, in danger from the Gentiles; danger in cities, danger in the wilderness, danger in the sea, danger among false brethren! I have met with toil and weariness, so often been sleepless, hungry and thirsty; so often denied myself food, gone cold and naked.

And all this, over and above something else which I do not count; I mean the burden I carry every day, my anxious care for all the churches; does anyone feel a scruple? I share it; is anyone's conscience hurt? I am ablaze with indignation.

If I must needs boast, I will boast of the things which humiliate me; the God who is Father of our Lord Jesus Christ, blessed be his name for ever, knows that I am telling the truth. When I was at Damascus, the agent of king Aretas was keeping guard over the city of the Damascenes, intent on seizing me, and to escape from his hands I had to be let down through a window along the wall, in a hamper. (2 Cor. 11: 22–33.)

There is an aspect of St. Paul and his career which we will venture to illustrate by reference to the work of Charlie Chaplin. Chaplin's work is so spiritually rich because it holds a mystery. His poetry consists in his miming of that dialectic which is a constant in the history of God's people: weakness overcoming strength to show the 'unexpectedness' of the Spirit and of God's wisdom. Charlie mimes Israel. From the days of Abraham, the father of emigrants, Israel, 'the smallest among all peoples', repeatedly demonstrated that law which was to continue to govern the life of the infant Church—a handful of Galileans, 'refuse of the world', against the imperial power of Rome, David against Goliath.

Paul understood the meaning of this dialectic of 'weakness' perfectly well; in the whole Bible, it is he who formulates it most exactly.

We have a treasure, then, in our keeping, but its shell is of perishable earthenware; it must be God, and not anything in ourselves, that gives it its sovereign power. (2 Cor. 4: 7.)

If we are to boast (although boasting is out of place), I will go on to the visions and revelations the Lord has granted me. There is a man I know who was carried out of himself in Christ, fourteen years since; was his spirit in his body? I cannot tell. Was it apart from his body? I cannot tell; God knows. This man, at least, was carried up into the third heaven. I can only tell you that this man, with his spirit in his body, or with his spirit apart from his body, God knows which, not I, was carried up into Paradise, and heard mysteries which man is not allowed to utter.

That is the man about whom I will boast; I will not boast about myself, except to tell you of my humiliations. It would not be vanity, if I had a mind to boast about such a man as that; I should only be telling the truth. But I will spare you the telling of it; I have no mind that anybody should think of me except as he sees me, as he hears me talking to him.

And indeed, for fear that these surpassing revelations should make me proud, I was given a sting to distress my outward nature, an angel of Satan sent to rebuff me. Three times it made me entreat the Lord to rid me of it; but he told me, 'My

'My grace is enough for thee; my strength finds its full scope in thy weakness' (2 Cor. 12: 9).
(Statue of Saint Paul in Saint-Trophime at Arles)

grace is enough for thee; my strength finds its full scope in thy weakness.'

More than ever, then, I delight to boast of the weaknesses that humiliate me, so that the strength of Christ may enshrine itself in me. I am well content with these humiliations of mine, with the insults, the hardships, the persecutions, the times of difficulty I undergo for Christ; when I am weakest, then I am strongest of all. (2 Cor. 12: 1–10.)

SHARING IN THE CROSS

The power of God is fulfilled in weakness and failure—it is this dialectic that best describes Paul's life, Christian life: participation in the mystery of Christ's cross. 'With Christ I hang upon the cross, and yet I am alive; or rather, not I; it is Christ that lives in me. . . . God forbid that I should make a display of anything, except the cross of our Lord Jesus Christ, through which the world stands crucified to me, and I to the world' (Gal. 2: 20; 6: 14).

The continuing actuality of the cross until the end of time would seem to be the essence of Paul's message. 'I am glad of my sufferings on your behalf, as, in this mortal frame of mine, I help to pay off the debt which the afflictions of Christ still leave to be paid, for the sake of his body, the Church' (Col. 1: 24); 'Be content, brethren, to follow my example, and mark well those who live by the pattern we have given them; I have told you often, and now tell you again with tears, that there are many whose lives make them the enemies of Christ's cross' (Phil. 3: 17–18).

We have a treasure, then, in our keeping, but its shell is of perishable earthenware; it must be God, and not anything in ourselves, that gives it its sovereign power. For ourselves, we are being hampered everywhere, yet still have room to breathe, are hard put to it, but never at a loss; persecution does not leave us unbefriended, nor crushing blows destroy us; we carry about continually in our bodies the dying state of Jesus, so that the living power of Jesus may be manifested in our bodies too. Always we, alive as we are, are being given up to death for Jesus' sake, so that the living power of Jesus may be manifested in this mortal nature of ours. So death makes itself felt in us, and life in you. . . .
Knowing that he who raised Jesus from the dead will raise us too, and summon us, like you, before him. . . .
No, we do not play the coward; though the outward part of our nature is being worn down, our inner life is refreshed from day to day. This light and momentary affliction brings with it a reward multiplied every way, loading us with everlasting glory; if only we will fix our eyes on what is unseen, not on what we can see. What we can see, lasts but for a moment; what is unseen is eternal. (2 Cor. 4: 7–12, 14, 16–18.)

The mystery of the Cross does not mean any unhealthy pre-occupation with suffering and death; it means a clear, sturdy consciousness of a world-wide truth, a law of creation: that if the grain does not fall into the ground and die, it remains alone. If it does fall into the ground and die, then it bears an abundant harvest. He who would save his soul—his life—will lose it; but he who assents to losing it will find it again, whole and more full than before.

We can verify this truth of the mystery of the Cross by an attentive examination of our own lives and of the lives of those whom we know, in the lives of individual persons as well as in the lives of peoples; it is the law that governs the economy of the life of the spirit.

A boat at Ostia
(Roman mosaic)

FROM JERUSALEM TO ROME
(in the year 59–60)

For St. Paul's arrest in Jerusalem, his imprisonment at Caesarea, and his journey to Rome, the reader must be referred to the Acts of the Apostles. It is sufficient here briefly to summarize the main facts.

The community at Jerusalem suggested that he should go into the Temple and give a public proof of his attachment to Judaism, in order to mollify the converted Jews who were accusing him of forsaking the Law of Moses. 'So, next day, Paul took the men [who were to fulfil a vow] with him, and began going to the temple, publicly fulfilling the days of purification . . .' (Acts 21: 26). And when the seven purification days were drawing to an end, the Asian Jews, seeing Paul in the Temple, stirred up the people and laid hands on him, shouting, 'Men of Israel, come to the rescue; here is the man who goes about everywhere, teaching everybody to despise our people, and our law and this place . . .' Seeing the tumult, the Roman tribune took Paul into custody, thus saving his life. He was allowed to address the crowd, and, in Aramaic, he told them about his life and conversion (Acts 22: 1–21; already quoted in full, pp. 28-30).

In order to learn exactly what the Jews accused Paul of, the tribune sent for the Sanhedrin and the chief priests, and brought his prisoner before them.

> And now, finding that there were two factions among them, one of the Sadducees and the other of the Pharisees, Paul cried out in the council, 'Brethren, I am a Pharisee, and my fathers were Pharisees before me. And I am standing on my trial because I am one who hopes for the resurrection of the dead.' When he said this, a dissension arose between the Pharisees and the Sadducees and the assembly was in two minds. The Sadducees will have it that there is no resurrection, that there are no angels or spirits, whereas the Pharisees believe in both. So that a great clamour followed; and some of the Pharisees came forward to protest; 'We cannot find any fault in this man', they said. 'Perhaps he has had a message from a spirit, or an angel.'
>
> Then dissension rose high; and the captain, who was afraid that they would tear Paul in pieces, ordered his troops to come down and rescue Paul from their midst, and bring him safe to the soldiers' quarters. On the next night, the Lord came to his side, and told him, 'Do not lose heart; thou hast done with bearing me witness in Jerusalem, and now thou must carry the same witness to Rome.' (Acts 23: 6–11.)

Some of the Jews laid a plot to kill Paul, and when the tribune heard this he had him removed under cover of night to Caesarea, to Felix, the procurator of Judaea. Here he was kept in prison for two years, till he was brought before Festus, who succeeded Felix in office. Hereupon, Paul appealed to Caesar, as was his right as a Roman citizen. 'You have appealed to Caesar?' said Festus, 'Then to Caesar you shall go.'

St. Luke was on that voyage, and in the Acts he gives a detailed account of it which has been called 'the most valuable maritime document of antiquity'. After being wrecked and wintering on Malta, they landed at last at Pozzuoli, near Naples: 'Here we found some brethren, who prevailed on us to stay with them for a week. And so we ended our journey at Rome. The brethren there, who had heard our story, came out as far as Appius'

Forum, and on to the Three Taverns, to meet us: Paul gave thanks to God and took courage when he saw them·

'Once we were in Rome, Paul was allowed to have his own residence, which he shared with the soldier who guarded him. ... And for two whole years he lived in a lodging hired at his own expense, and welcomed all who came to visit him, proclaiming God's kingdom, and teaching them the truths which concern our Lord Jesus Christ, boldly enough, without let or hindrance' (Acts 28: 14–16, 30–31). Thus ends the book of Acts of the Apostles.

During this time of detention Paul had around him Luke, 'the beloved physician', Mark, cousin to Barnabas and Paul's fellow worker, and many others, brethren from Thessalonica, Colossae, Ephesus and Philippi. From Rome it was that Paul sent out those great letters called the Epistles of the Captivity, to the Colossians, the Ephesians and the Philippians, letters that are the final synthesis of his theology and mysticism, in which his knowledge of the mystery of Christ is seen in all its height and depth. It is these letters that we began by quoting.

St. Paul's last years are a much discussed historical problem; with the ending of the book of Acts we are left only with a series of conjectures. No discussion of the exegetical problems involved can be undertaken in such a short biographical sketch as this.

If the authenticity of the Pastoral Epistles be admitted, one is led to think that Paul was set free after the burning of Rome in the year 64, and that he undertook a last missionary journey. We learn from the Epistle to the Romans (15: 24, 28) that he had intended for some time to visit Spain; certain words of Clement of Rome—'He went to the frontiers of the West'—are interpreted by some as meaning he actually did so. According to his first letter to Timothy (1: 3), he will have passed through Ephesus on the way to Macedonia; Titus (1: 5) implies he was in Crete, and 2 Timothy (4: 13 and 20) that he was again at Troas and Miletus. The last-named letter was written from Rome; Paul was again a prisoner.

'Brethren came out as far as Appius' Forum, and on to the Three Taverns, to meet us' (Acts 28: 15)

'In Asia, as thou knowest, all have treated me coldly. . . . May the Lord grant mercy to the household of Onesiphorus; often enough he revived my spirits. Instead of being ashamed of a prisoner's acquaintance, he sought me out when he was in Rome, and succeeded in finding me. . . .

'At my first trial, no one stood by me: I was deserted by everybody; may it be forgiven them. But the Lord was at my side; he endowed me with strength, so that through me the preaching of the gospel might attain its full scope, and all the Gentiles might hear it; thus I was brought safely out of the jaws of the lion.

'Yes, the Lord has preserved me from every assault of evil; he will bring me safely into his heavenly kingdom; glory be to him through endless ages, Amen' (2 Tim. 1: 15–17; 4: 16–18).

Nothing is known for certain about the end of Paul's life. There is an unanimous tradition that he was martyred in Rome under Nero, but there is no information about the date or the circumstances. He was buried beside the road to Ostia.

Martyrdom of Saint Paul (window at Le Mans)

Death is an *action*, and one co-extensive with the whole life-time of a Christian: a sharing of Christ's death, an experiencing of his cross, by which we receive an earnest of the resurrection. 'Risen, then, with Christ, you must lift your thoughts above, where Christ now sits at the right hand of God. . . . You have undergone death, and your life is hidden away now with Christ in God. Christ is your life, and when he is made manifest, you too will be made manifest in glory with him' (Col. 3: 1–4).

From the time when the crucified and risen Christ appeared to him, Paul so to say lived the act of death; it only remained for him to complete and perfect this act of fellowship in Christ's death. 'As for me, my blood already flows in sacrifice; the time has nearly come when I can go free. I have fought the good fight; I have finished the race; I have redeemed my pledge; I look forward to the prize that is waiting for me, the prize I have earned. The Lord, the judge whose award never goes amiss, will grant it to me when that day comes; to me, yes, and all those who have learned to welcome his appearing' (2 Tim. 4: 6–8). He had previously written to the Philippians (1: 20–24): '. . . this body of mine will do Christ honour, now as always, in life or in death. For me, life means Christ; death is a prize to be won. But what if living on in this mortal body is the only way to harvest what I have sown? Thus I cannot tell what to choose; I am hemmed in on both sides. I long to have done with it, and be with Christ, a better thing, much more than a better thing; and yet, for your sakes, that I should wait in the body is more urgent still.'

Just as, in the thought of the primitive Church, love did not mean what it does in the language of today and of 'tales of love and death', so, in the mind of Paul, death did not have the meaning that it takes on nowadays under the influence of philosophies of 'being-in-order-to-die'. For the world, death is a synonym for nothingness; the world's pathos is the sadness of being, only to die.

Following Paul, we have to break up this association of death with nothingness, so that it may be seen as an action which enables us to share Christ's resurrection, 'if only we share his sufferings'. To die is not synonymous with 'to cease to be', but with 'to be for Christ'. 'While we live, we live as the Lord's servants, when we die, we die as the Lord's servants; in life and in death, *we belong* to the Lord. That was why Christ died and lived again; he would be Lord both of the dead and of the living' (Rom. 14: 8–9). At the very beginning of his missionary labours, Paul wrote about this to the Thessalonians (1, 4: 12–13): 'Make no mistake, brethren, about those who have gone to their rest; you are not to lament over them, as the rest of the world does, with no hope to live by. We believe, after all, that Jesus underwent death and rose again; just so, when Jesus comes back, God will bring back those who have found rest through him.'

'We believe that Jesus underwent death and rose again' (1 Thess. 4: 13). (*Autun*)

'The Lord is near' (Phil. 4: 5)

'The Last Judgement' from The Book of Piety,
(13th century)

JOY

St. Paul generally writes of joy in the context of persecution.

... as God's ministers, we must do everything to make ourselves acceptable. We have to shew great patience, in times of affliction, of need, of difficulty; under the lash, in prison, in the midst of tumult; when we are tired out, sleepless, and fasting. We have to be pure-minded, enlightened, forgiving and gracious to others; we have to rely on the Holy Spirit, on unaffected love, on the truth of our message, on the power of God. To right and to left we must be armed with innocence; now honoured, now slighted, now traduced, now flattered. They call us deceivers, and we tell the truth; unknown, and we are fully acknowledged; dying men, and see, we live; punished, yes, but not doomed to die; sad men, that rejoice continually; beggars, that bring riches to many; disinherited, and the world is ours. (2 Cor. 6: 4–10.)

But it is in the Epistle to the Philippians, without doubt written from Rome ('in my imprisonment', he says) that Paul talks most about joy, and most often urges it on his children.

I hasten to assure you, brethren, that my circumstances here have only had the effect of spreading the gospel further; so widely has my imprisonment become known, in Christ's honour, throughout the praetorium and to all the world beyond. And most of the brethren, deriving fresh confidence in the Lord from my imprisonment, are making bold to preach God's word with more freedom than ever.

Some of them, it is true, for no better reason than rivalry or jealousy; but there are others who really proclaim Christ out of good will. Some, I mean, are moved by charity, because they recognize that I am here to defend the gospel, others by party spirit, proclaiming Christ from wrong motives, just because they hope to make my chains gall me worse. What matter, so long as either way, for private ends or in all honesty, Christ is proclaimed? Of that I am glad now; yes, and I shall be glad hereafter. (Phil. 1: 12–18.)

Though your faith should prove to be a sacrifice which cannot be duly made without my blood for its drink-offering, I congratulate myself and all of you over that; on your side, you too must congratulate yourselves and me. (Phil. 2: 17–18.)

And now, brethren, joy to you in the Lord. (Phil. 3: 1.)

Joy to you in the Lord at all times; once again I wish you joy . . . The Lord is near. Nothing must make you anxious; in every need make your requests known to God, praying and beseeching him, and giving him thanks as well. So may the peace of God, which surpasses all our thinking, watch over your hearts and minds in Christ Jesus. (Phil. 4: 4–7.)

THE MYSTERY OF ANTICHRIST

An account of St. Paul's vision of the world cannot be left without any reference to the negative element in the story. In actual history, God's work meets opposition, not only individually from each one of us, but social, organized, political opposition. Face to face with the City of God, being built up of living stones, there stands a hostile city, spiritually called Babylon.

The creation of a holy mankind, called to be like God, begins with a particular people, which grows like the big tree of which the gospels speak, or, again, works like leaven to transform the

179

'*The champion of wickedness must appear first*' (2 *Thess.* 2: 3).
('*The Beast of the Apocalypse*' *from* The Book of Piety)

lump. But in the course of her history Israel met bitter opposition from other peoples, who followed one another in resisting the chosen of God. Certain men stand out as leaders in this struggle with Israel: Pharaoh, Sennacherib, Nebuchadnezzar, Antiochus Epiphanes, Pompey and others.

The prophets understood this conflict in accordance with the perpetual dialectic that has been set forth. Israel occupies the Promised Land, and then forgets the Lord her God. Whereupon God raises up a people to chastise Israel, lest she be swallowed up in the void of idolatry and wickedness. The prophets called these peoples 'Yahweh's rod' or 'Yahweh's hammer'; they were

the instruments of his wrath; or, more exactly, God used the nations' hatred of Israel for the correction of his beloved people. But those nations were to be chastised in their turn.

Actually, this hatred of Israel was hatred of God's work itself, which was being carried out through his people. The nations rose up against the Lord and against his anointed—the king of Israel. Thus the idea of an Antichrist was born.

When the Church appeared on the scene, this hostility to the people of God took on a twofold character, while still remaining the same thing. It is manifested by hatred of Israel, the Jewish people ('anti-semitism'), and by hatred of the Church. The two go together: hostile men and parties detect or divine God's work in the one as in the other. By a sure instinct, the Caesars of all times—whether they be individuals or 'collectivities'—recognize in God's people a principle incompatible with their own tyranny. From Nero to Hitler the same spirit is at work, provoking war to the death against the Church and against the dispersed of Israel. Some Christian theologians may fail to recognize Antichrist, but Antichrist never fails to recognize the deep inner unity of the people of God.

The distinguishing mark of this people is justice and holiness; but the Prince of Babylon is always known by his cruelty, his obscenity, his taste for magic and spell-binding. Even individual characteristics are alike: in Nero as in Hitler we see the same relish for the blood and terror of tragedy—'the comic tragedians' —which will even reduce the city, the world, to ruins to feed its lusts. The prophets proclaimed that in the course of its history mankind would keep on giving rein to this evil power that it carries within itself. History will be consummated in a war between the two camps, the people of God and their adversary. That people is now found in every corner of the earth: Babylon is no longer simply the city on the river—its ruler is now called the Prince of this world. The drama is worldwide.

There is no need, brethren, to write to you about the times and the seasons of all this; you are keeping it clearly in mind, without being told, that the day of the Lord will come like a thief in the night. It is just when men are saying, All quiet,

Ezekiel's vision of the deliverance of Israel and the rising of the dead (Byzantine manuscript, 9th century)

all safe, that doom will fall upon them suddenly, like the pangs that come to a woman in travail, and there will be no escape from it. Whereas you, brethren, are not living in the darkness, for the day to take you by surprise, like a thief; no, you are all born to the light, born to the day; we do not belong to the night and its darkness. We must not sleep on, then, like the rest of the world, we must watch and keep sober. (1 Thess. 5: 1–6.)

St. Paul returns to this matter of the Lord's coming, in his second letter to the same church.

But there is one entreaty we would make of you, brethren, as you look forward to the time when our Lord Jesus Christ will come, and gather us in to himself. Do not be terrified out of your senses all at once, and thrown into confusion, by any spiritual utterance, any message or letter purporting to come from us, which suggests that the day of the Lord is close at hand. Do not let anyone find the means of leading you astray. The apostasy must come first; the champion of wickedness must appear first, destined to inherit perdition. This is the rebel who is to lift up his head above every divine name, above all that men hold in reverence, till at last he enthrones himself in God's temple, and proclaims himself as God.

Do not you remember my telling you of this, before I left your company? At present there is a power (you know what I mean) which holds him in check, so that he may not shew himself before the time appointed to him; meanwhile, the conspiracy of revolt is already at work; only, he who checks it now will be able to check it, until he is removed from the enemy's path. Then it is that the rebel will shew himself; and the Lord Jesus will destroy him with the breath of his mouth, overwhelming him with the brightness of his presence. He will come, when he comes, with all Satan's influence to aid him; there will be no lack of power, of counterfeit signs and wonders; and his wickedness will deceive the souls that are doomed, to punish them for refusing that fellowship in the truth which would have saved them. That is why God is letting loose among them a deceiving influence, so that they give credit to falsehood; he will single out for judgement all those who refused credence to the truth, and took their pleasure in wrong-doing. (2 Thess. 2: 1–11.)

'The Lord Jesus shall destroy the rebel
with the breath of his mouth'
2 Thess. 2: 8. (Daphni)

The work of God will be complete when man shall have come to the fullness of his age, when he shall have reached the term of his supernatural and transfiguring vocation, the calling to share in the life of the Triune God. It is in Christ and through Christ that young mankind is begotten, transformed, ransomed, so that it may become capable of God's life, in accordance with the prophetic words, 'Let us make man, wearing our own image and likeness.'

'Some he has appointed to be apostles, others to be prophets, others to be evangelists, or pastors, or teachers. They are to order the lives of the faithful, minister to their needs, build up the frame of Christ's body, until we all realize our common unity through faith in the Son of God, and fuller knowledge of him. So we shall reach perfect manhood, that maturity which is proportioned to the completed growth of Christ' (Eph. 4: 11–13).

We may accordingly legitimately speak of a divinization of man in and through Christ: mankind consecrated and raised to the height of the temple of God. Without confusion of persons or surrender of our eternal and inalienable name, but with all the delightfulness of variety, the total *Adam* is transformed, made supernatural, that it may be the Body of Christ: 'God all in all. . . . Christ all and in all'. This consecration, this supernaturalizing, this assimilation to God is the consummation of the divine work. It is this that St. Paul calls the Fullness (*pleroma*).

And it is from this standpoint of incorporation in Christ that the Lord's Supper is to be understood.

> The tradition which I received from the Lord, and handed on to you, is that the Lord Jesus, on the night when he was being betrayed, took bread, and gave thanks, and broke it, and said, 'Take, eat; this is my body, given up for you. Do this for a commemoration of me.'
>
> And so with the cup, when supper was ended, 'This cup,' he said, 'is the new testament, in my blood. Do this, whenever you drink it, for a commemoration of me.'

'The grace of our Lord Jesus Christ be with you all'
2 *Thess.* 3: 18. (*Chartres*)

So it is the Lord's death that you are heralding, whenever you eat this bread and drink this cup, until he comes.

And therefore, if anyone eats this bread or drinks this cup of the Lord unworthily, he will be held to account for the Lord's body and blood. A man must examine himself first, and then eat of that bread and drink of that cup; he is eating and drinking damnation to himself if he eats and drinks unworthily, not recognizing the Lord's body for what it is. (I Cor. 11: 23–29.)

LORD, COME!

That letter to the Corinthians was dictated, but Paul wrote its ending himself: 'I send you', he says, 'my greetings in my own handwriting, PAUL'. May we be allowed to finish this essay with words with which he concluded his letters to the communities he had begotten in the Lord?

> If there is anyone who has no love for the Lord, let him be held accursed; the Lord is coming.
>
> The grace of our Lord Jesus Christ, and the love of God, and the imparting of the Holy Spirit be with you all.
>
> AMEN.

The Fish Symbol: ΙΧΘΥΣ

*Christ with Paul
and Peter
(5th century ivory)*

BIBLIOGRAPHICAL NOTE

Whoever knows even only a little Greek is most strongly urged to get a Greek New Testament and to make a habit of reading St. Paul's letters, and all the New Testament, in their original language. To do this is to make a discovery, in the exact meaning of that word, an unveiling. Away goes dust that has accumulated on the sacred text over the centuries, the 'pious noises' whose unconsidered familiarity lulls the mind to sleep, all the funereal wrappings that have got wound round the inspired words. The reader finds himself carried away into the clear light of Galilee, he breathes the air of the Judaean hills. Words and phrases that we think we understand, because we have heard them so often, take on their native, their real, meaning.

There are pitfalls in *any* translation. We find *Khristos* rendered as 'Christ', *euaggelion* as 'gospel', *ekklesia* as 'church', *apostolos* as 'apostle', *aggelos* as 'angel', and so on: which means that, instead of the Greek being translated, Greek words have been left in Greek, or translated by English words whose real meaning has been forgotten (gospel = good news). God's word has become a cryptogram, and only the learned have got the key.

And then there is that corruption of the significance of words which has helped to bring about a slackening in spiritual tension: it has been remarked in the course of this book what has happened to *agape*. There are plenty of other expressions that have suffered a similar fate: *oikodomein*, which in St. Paul signifies to build up, to build together (the Body of Christ), is translated by 'edify'; the Greek term which means to proclaim or announce the good news of God's word becomes 'to preach'; and we may recall here that unfortunate expression The 'Sermon' on the Mount.

For English-speaking readers, mention may be made of *The Student's New Testament* (Cambridge and Chicago, 1954), which has Westcott and Hort's Greek text and a translation by Edgar J. Goodspeed. In the present translation of M. Tresmontant's book, verbatim quotations from the Bible are given in Mgr. Ronald Knox's version, by kind permission of his Grace the Archbishop of Westminster, Messrs. Burns Oates & Washbourne Ltd., and Messrs. Sheed and Ward, Inc. The following is a selection of books recommended as complementary reading to the present statement of St. Paul's theological thought.

J. BONSIRVEN, *Le Judaïsme palestinien au temps de Jésus-Christ* (Paris, 1935).

P. BOYLAN, *St. Paul's Epistle to the Romans* (Dublin, 1934).

F. CUMONT, *Lux perpetua* (Paris, 1949).

W. P. DAVIES, *Paul and Rabbinic Judaism* (London, 1948).

A. Deissmann, *Paul: a Study in Social and Religious History* (London, 1926). Now available in Torchbooks (New York, 1957).
— *Light from the Ancient East* (New York, 1946).

A. J. Festugière, *Le monde gréco-romain au temps de Notre Seigneur* (2 vols, Paris, 1935).

A. H. N. Green-Armytage, *A Portrait of St. Luke* (London, 1955), Chapter VI and *passim*.

R. A. Knox, *St. Paul's Gospel* (London, 1950).

C. Lattey, *St. Paul and His Teaching* (London, 1930).

J. Lebreton and J. Zeiller, *The History of the Primitive Church*, Vol. I (London, 1949).

H. Lietzmann, *History of the Early Church*, Vol. I (London, 1951).

H. V. Morton, *In the Steps of St. Paul* (London, 1949).

F. Prat, *The Theology of St. Paul* (2 vols, London, 1927–34).

W. M. Ramsay, *St. Paul the Traveller and Roman Citizen* (London, 1895).
— *The Cities of St. Paul, their Influence on his Life and Thought* (London, 1907).

G. Ricciotti, *Paul the Apostle* (Milwaukee, 1953).

J. W. C. Wand, *The New Testament Letters* (Oxford, 1946).

ILLUSTRATIONS

Éliane Janet - Le Caisne: 2, 51, 78, 86, 167, 176.
Élienne Houvet (Chartres): 44, 48, 184.
Jean Roubier: 138.
R. P. Benoît (École Biblique de Jérusalem): 66, 76, 127a.
R. P. Grollenberg (Atlas de la Bible): 24, 27, 90a, 90b.
H. Metzger: 134, 141.
R. Matton: 136.
Bibliothèque Nationale: 64, 70, 77, 149, 164, 180.
Semitic Museum (Harvard University): 39.
John Rylands Library: 12.
Cambridge University Library: 19.
Archives Photo: 25, 46, 53, 60, 113, 121, 156, 174.
Roger-Viollet: 17, 84, 92, 105, 106, 128, 186.
Roger-Viollet-Alinari: 26, 28, 152.
Roger-Viollet-Anderson: 29, 54, 172.
Giraudon: 23, 81, 88, 133b, 177, 179.
Giraudon-Alinari: 8a, 9c.
Giraudon-Anderson: 1 cv, 34a, 35, 36, 37, 120, 133a, 142, 170.
Bulloz: 139.
Roger Roche: 95, 98, 101, 110, 155, 168.
Jean Denis (*Saintes*): 9a, 9b.

Ricciotti: Saint Paul Apôtre (Éditions Robert Laffont, Paris, 1952): 6a, 34b, 91.
Morton: Sur les pas de Saint Paul (Éditions Hachette, Paris): 16, 93a, 93b, 127b.
Deismann: Paul, a study in social and religious history (Hodder and Stoughton, London, 1926): 129, 135.
Cecchelli: Iconografia dei Papi: 2 cv, 109, 187, 3 cv.
Wilpert: Die Malereien der Katakomben Roms: 22, 155.
Wilpert: Die Mosaïken und Malereien der kirchlichen Bauten: 101, 110, 168.
Atlas de la Bible (Éditions Elsevier, Paris-Bruxelles, 1955): 7a.
Laffont-Bompiani: Dictionnaire des Œuvres (S. E. D. E.): 75.
Henri Michel: Histoire de l'Art. II, 1. (Éditions Armand Colin, Paris): 40, 146, 150.
Emile Mâle: L'Art religieux du XIIᵉ siècle en France (Éditions Armand Colin, Paris, 1947): 43.
Würthwein: Der Text des Alten Testaments (Württ, Bibelanstalt, Stuttgart, 1952): 11.

LONGMANS, GREEN AND CO LTD
48 GROSVENOR STREET, LONDON W I
RAILWAY CRESCENT, CROYDON, VICTORIA, AUSTRALIA
AUCKLAND, KINGSTON (JAMAICA), LAHORE, NAIROBI
LONGMANS SOUTHERN AFRICA (PTY) LTD
THIBAULT HOUSE, THIBAULT SQUARE, CAPE TOWN
JOHANNESBURG, SALISBURY
LONGMANS OF NIGERIA LTD
W. R. INDUSTRIAL ESTATE, IKEJA
LONGMANS OF GHANA LTD
INDUSTRIAL ESTATE, RING ROAD SOUTH, ACCRA
LONGMANS GREEN (FAR EAST) LTD
443 LOCKHART ROAD, HONG KONG
LONGMANS OF MALAYA LTD
44 JALAN AMPANG, KUALA LUMPUR
ORIENT LONGMANS LTD
CALCUTTA, BOMBAY, MADRAS
DELHI, HYDERABAD, DACCA
LONGMANS CANADA LTD
137 BOND STREET, TORONTO 2

HARPER AND BROTHERS
49 EAST 33RD STREET
NEW YORK 16

LIBRARY OF CONGRESS CATALOG CARD NUMBER: 58-5220

*First published in France
by Editions du Seuil, Paris*

This edition first published 1957
Third impression 1962

TYPE SET BY WESTERN PRINTING SERVICES LTD., BRISTOL.
PRINTED IN GREAT BRITAIN BY LOWE AND BRYDONE
(PRINTERS) LTD. NIHIL OBSTAT JOANNES M. T. BARTONS,
S.T.D., L.S.S. CENSOR DEPUTATUS. IMPRIMATUR E. MORROGH
BERNARD VIC. GEN. WESTMONASTERII, DIE 28A, JUNII, 1957.

Tresmontant, Claude

St. Paul and the mystery
of Christ

227   T   5170